For me, the wine experience is composed of more than just wine in the glass; it is a sensory experience that elevates the everyday by inviting you to slow down and become part of the moment. What I try to capture in all of my paintings is the natural way we go about sharing wine with friends... the moment when people feel good.

This journal is my personal invitation to join me in creating those moments. The occasion can be a wedding, an anniversary or just a Saturday evening. Spark a great conversation as you share a bottle with friends or enjoy a glass as you while away the afternoon. Whether you are making new memories or celebrating old ones, the best luxuries in life are meant to be shared.

Cheers,

ARVID

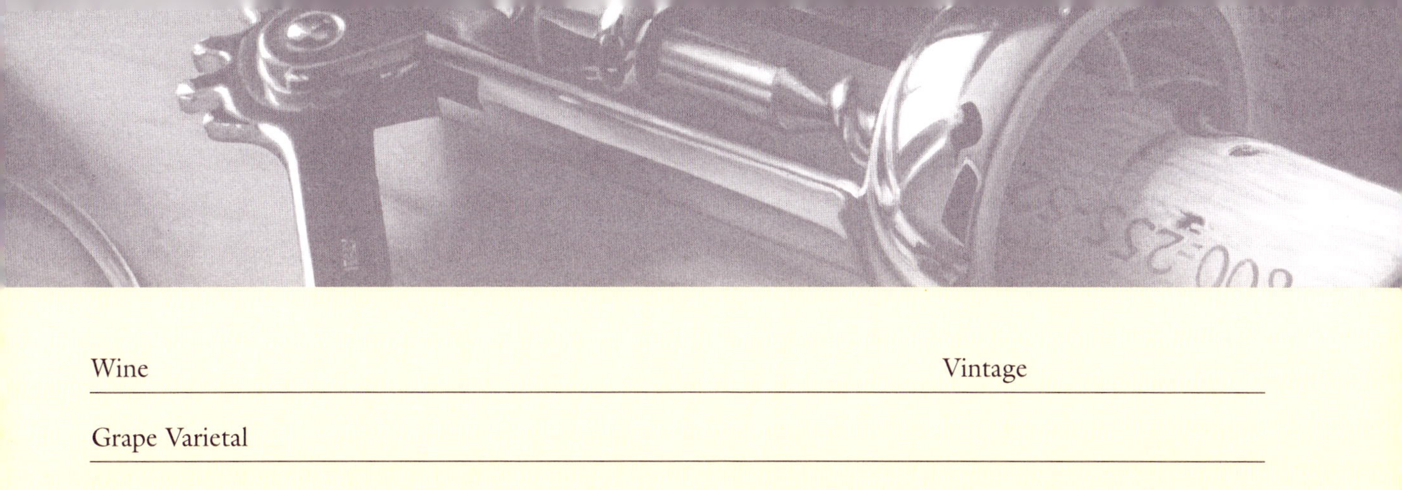

Wine Vintage

Grape Varietal

Purchase Details

Shared With

Occasion

Date

Flavors

Finish

Notes

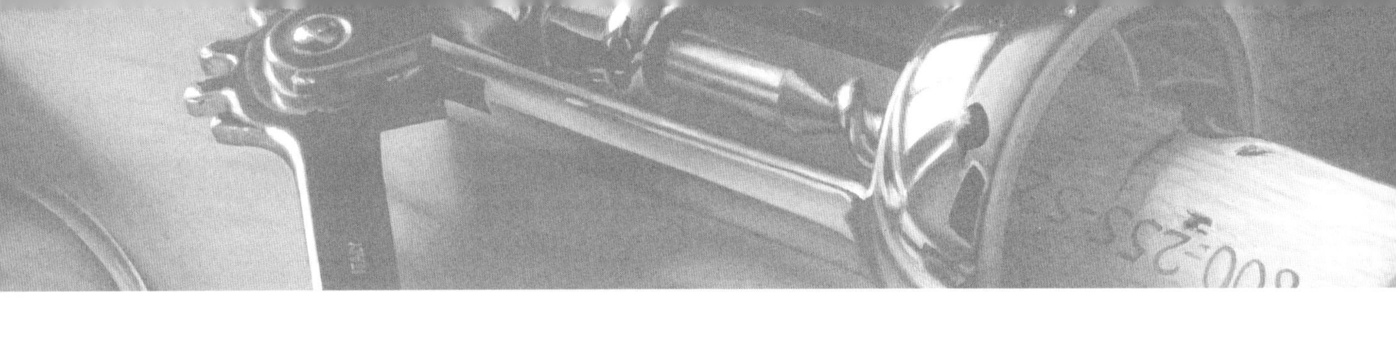

Wine Vintage

Grape Varietal

Purchase Details

Shared With

Occasion

Date

Flavors

Finish

Notes

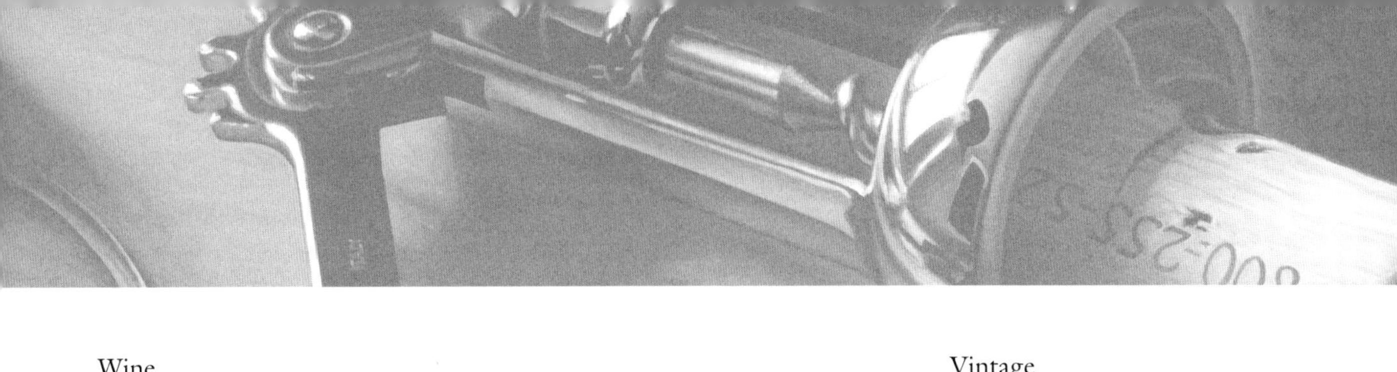

Wine Vintage

Grape Varietal

Purchase Details

Shared With

Occasion

Date

Flavors

Finish

Notes

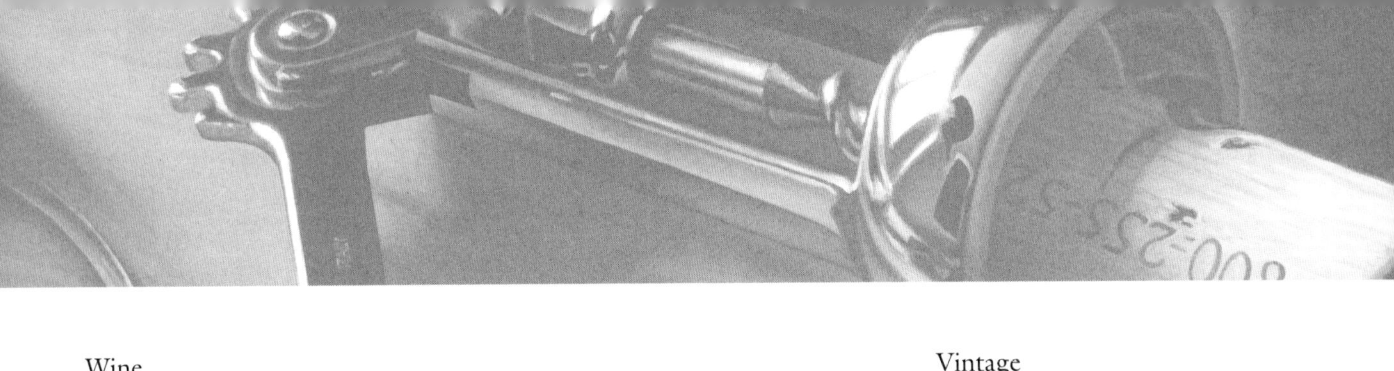

Wine Vintage

Grape Varietal

Purchase Details

Shared With

Occasion

Date

Flavors

Finish

Notes

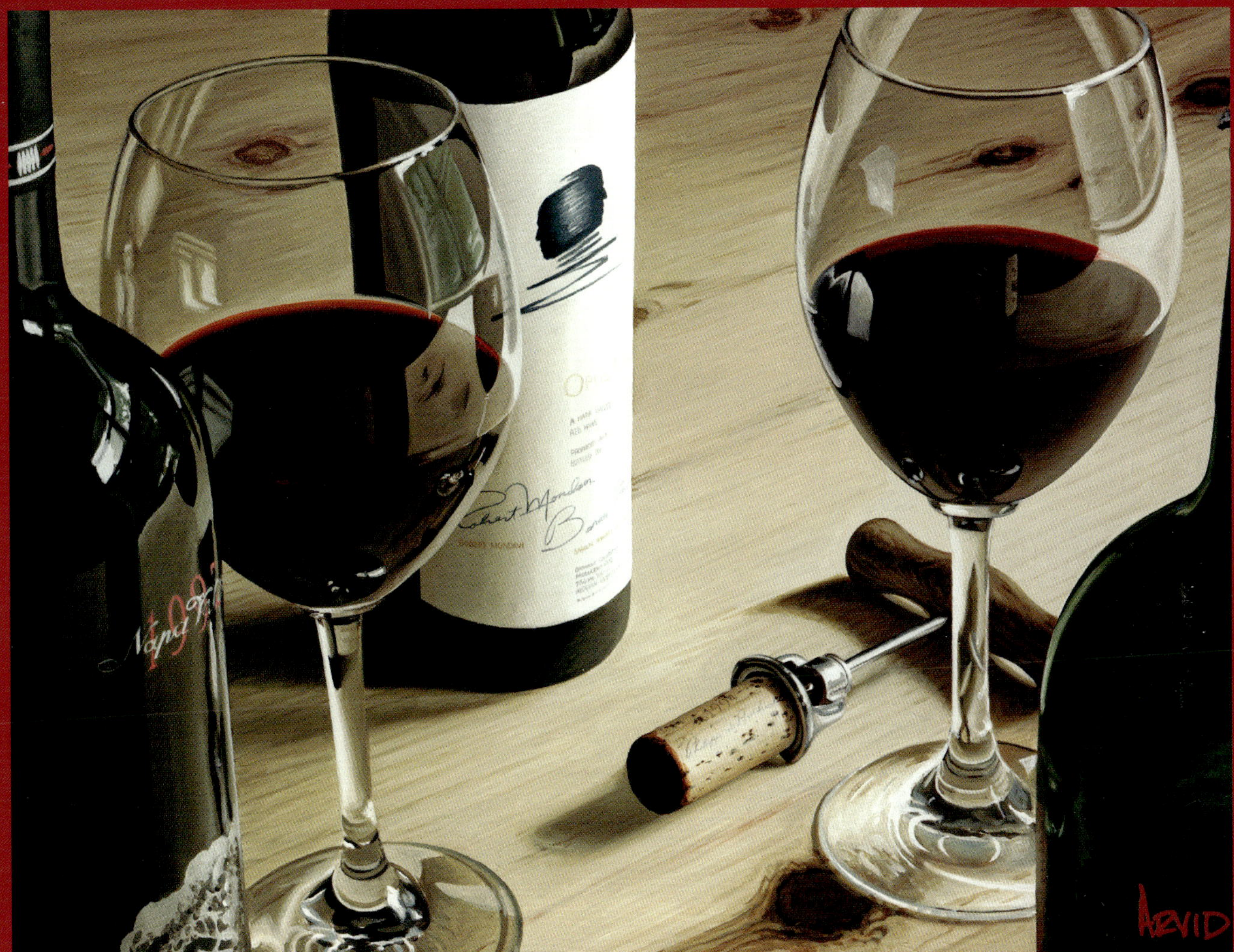

Oakville Crossing

Named for one of Napa Valley's famous side roads, *Oakville Crossing* shows the intersection of several bottles of spectacular wine. In an equally spectacular composition, Arvid once again stuns us with his facility for capturing not just light and color but specific, if fleeting, moments in time. In this case, it's that moment we savor of both appreciation for what's in our glass and anticipation for what's yet to come.

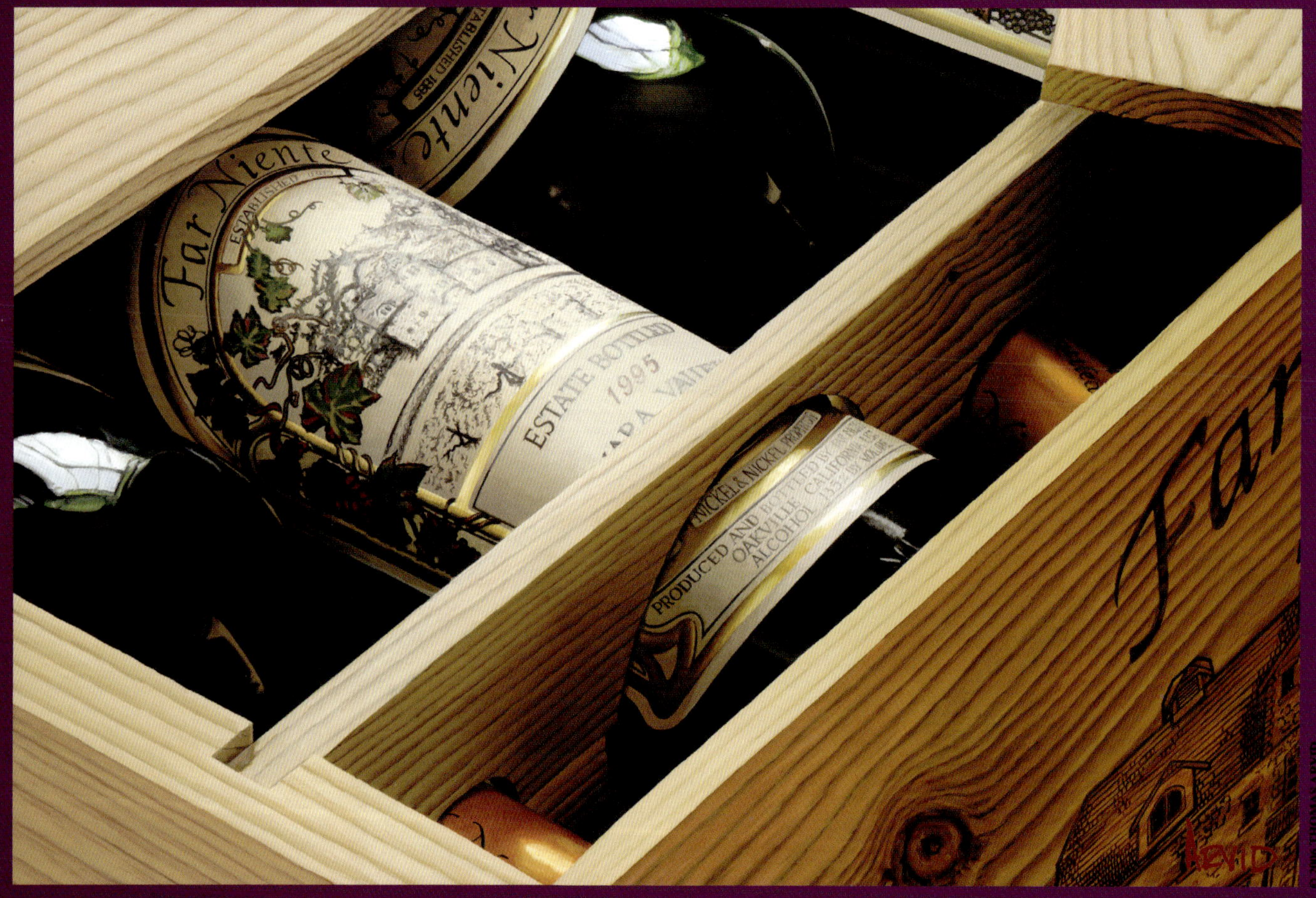

Best Case Scenario

Truly a collector, Arvid describes the arrival of a new case of wine: "It's like Christmas morning; whether it's to stock the cellar or to drink it, there's beauty in the feeling that you get when you open a case of wine." The curve of the bottles and the finely detailed labels both contrast and echo the hard edges and the soft grain of the wood crate, inviting you to explore each subtle nuance and shadow. Sharply in focus, *Best Case Scenario* parallels Arvid's artistic growth and transition. By continually finding new angles and approaches to his subject, Arvid constantly raises the bar for his talent and his work.

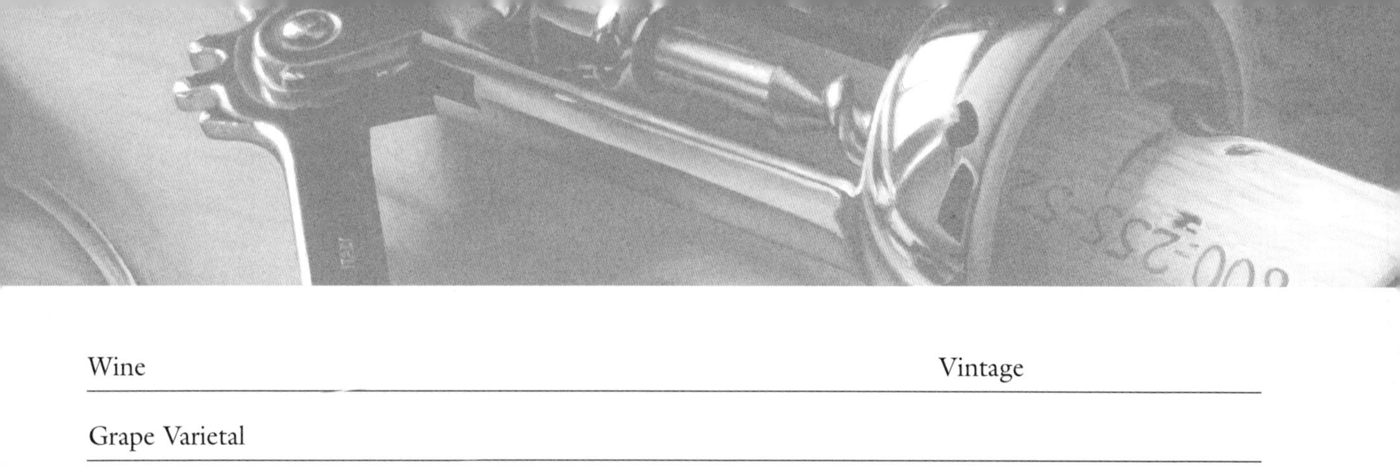

Wine	Vintage

Grape Varietal

Purchase Details

Shared With

Occasion

Date

Flavors

Finish

Notes

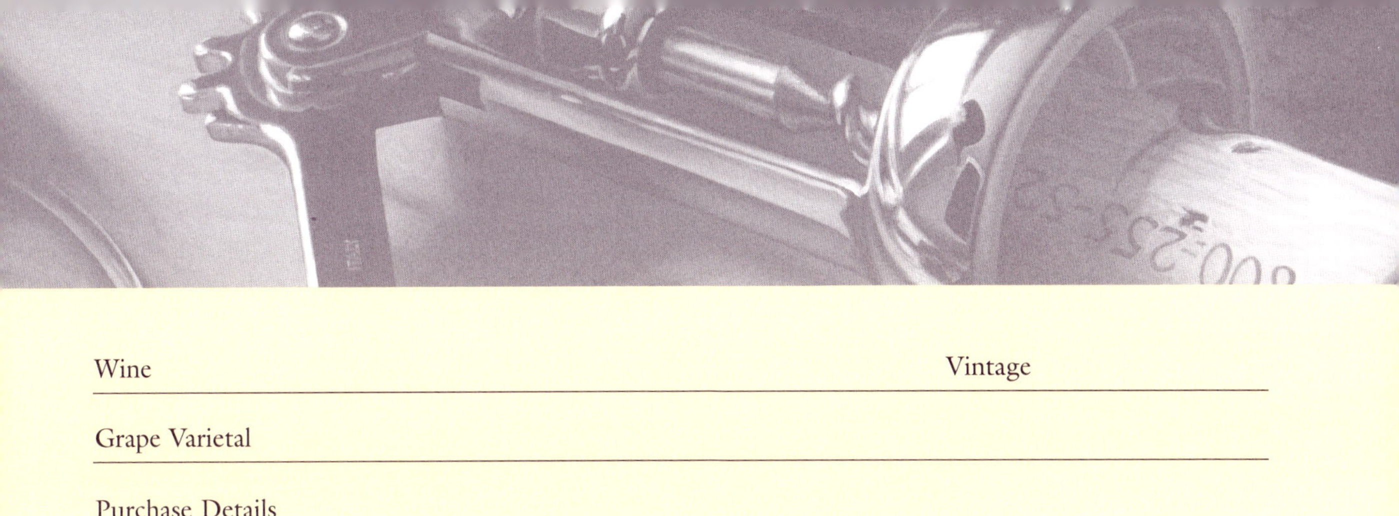

Wine Vintage

Grape Varietal

Purchase Details

Shared With

Occasion

Date

Flavors

Finish

Notes

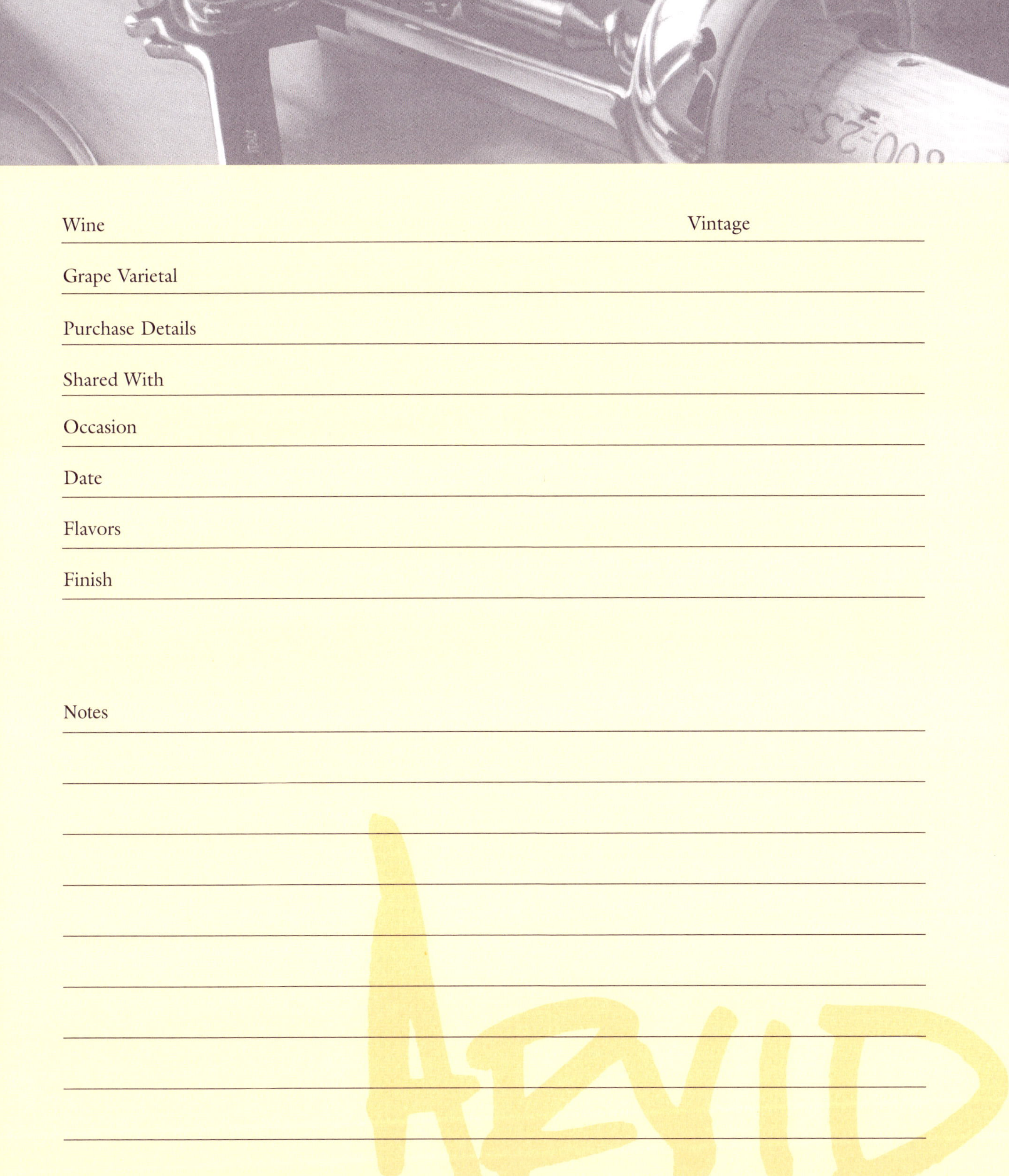

Wine Vintage

Grape Varietal

Purchase Details

Shared With

Occasion

Date

Flavors

Finish

Notes

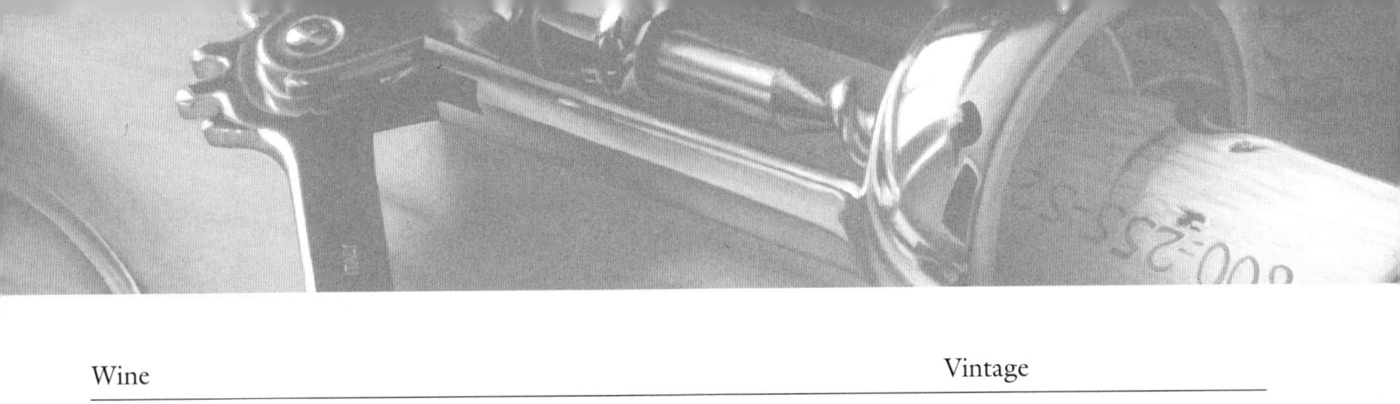

Wine ______________________________ Vintage ______________

Grape Varietal ______________________________

Purchase Details ______________________________

Shared With ______________________________

Occasion ______________________________

Date ______________________________

Flavors ______________________________

Finish ______________________________

Notes ______________________________

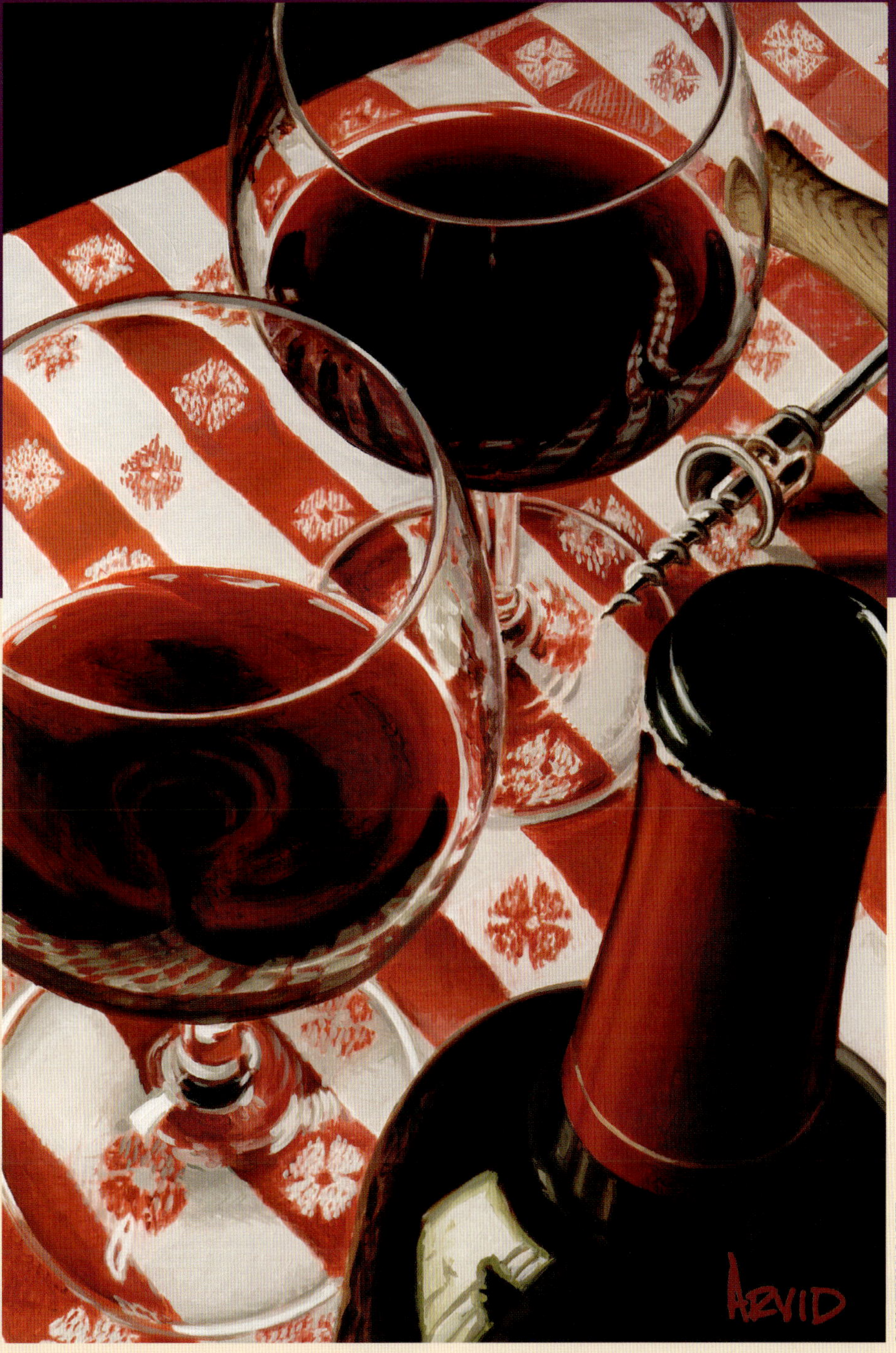

Red and White Table

"In this, my first painting of wine, I set out to capture the reality of drinking wine. *Red & White Table* breaks all the rules of what was seen previously in wine paintings and still lifes. People gravitate to it because it is immediate, and they relate to it." *—Arvid*

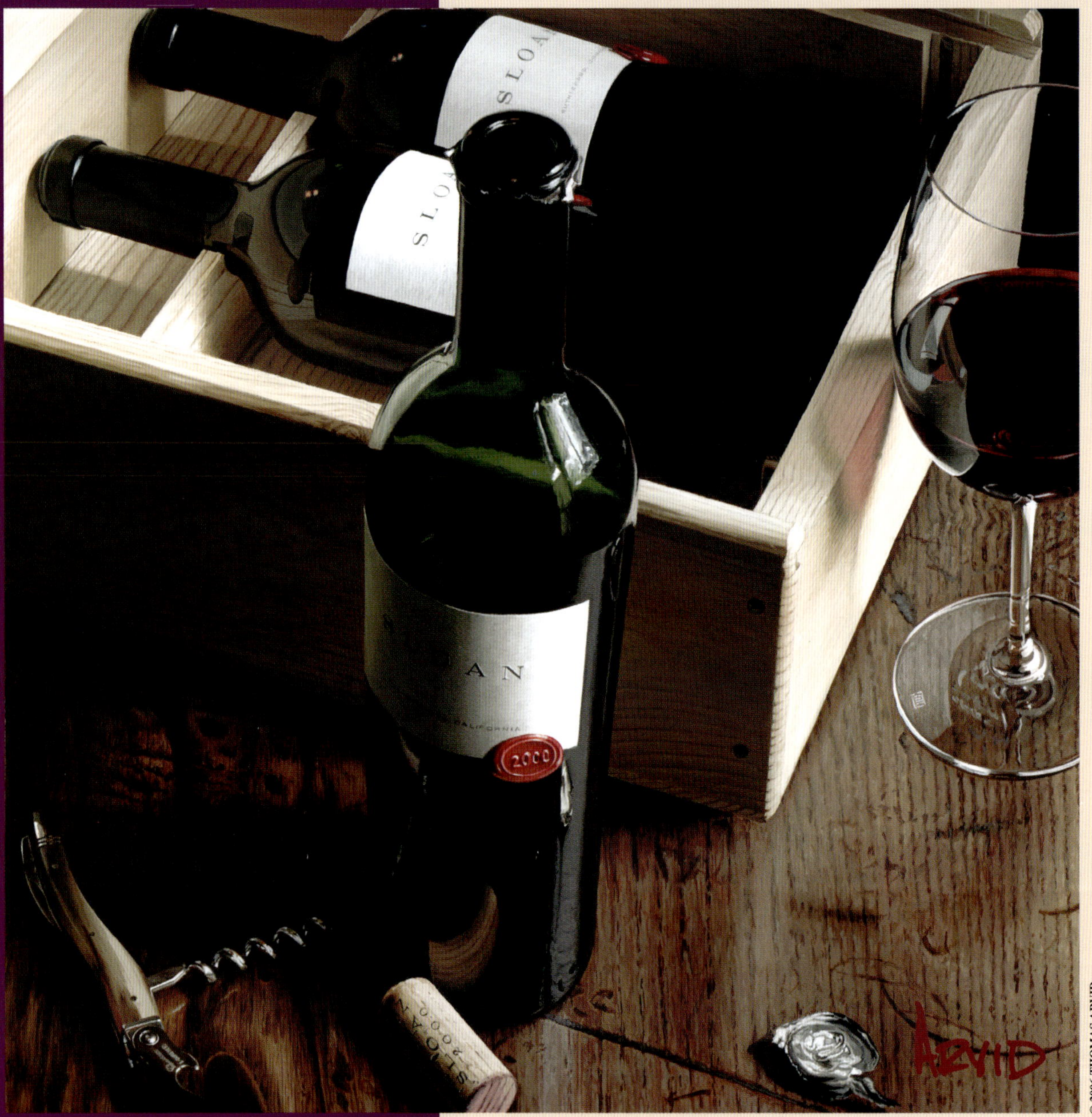

A Notch Above

"Years ago, I donated one of my paintings to a charitable auction and the person who bought it actually gave it back to me! He was a budding winemaker in the process of making his first vintage and wanted to make a trade: 'When my wine is ready, I want you to paint it.' Two years passed and I finally got an invitation to Sloan Vineyards. As soon as I experienced the first taste, I knew this had to be a special piece. The fine detail of craftsmanship and commitment to excellence in the wine inspired me." *—Arvid*

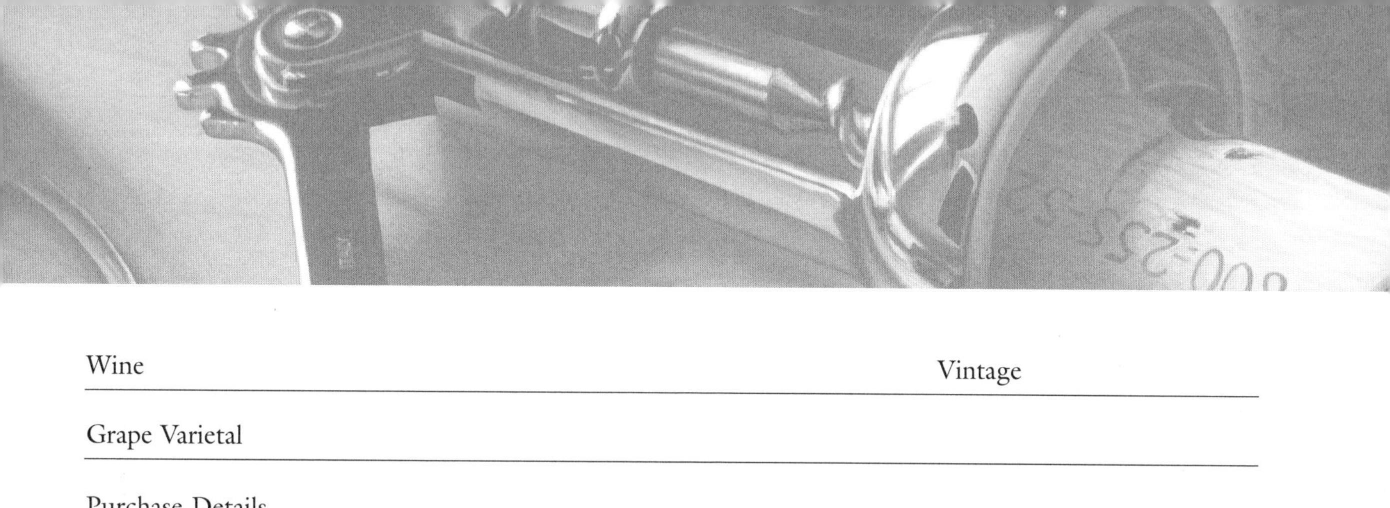

Wine Vintage

Grape Varietal

Purchase Details

Shared With

Occasion

Date

Flavors

Finish

Notes

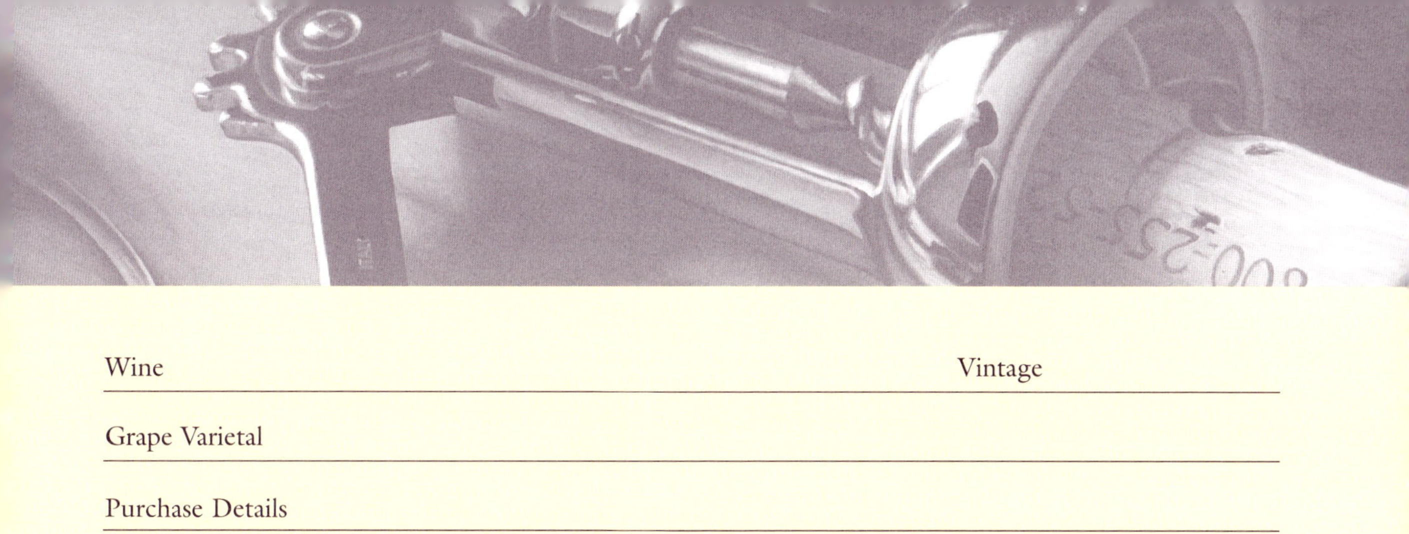

Wine Vintage

Grape Varietal

Purchase Details

Shared With

Occasion

Date

Flavors

Finish

Notes

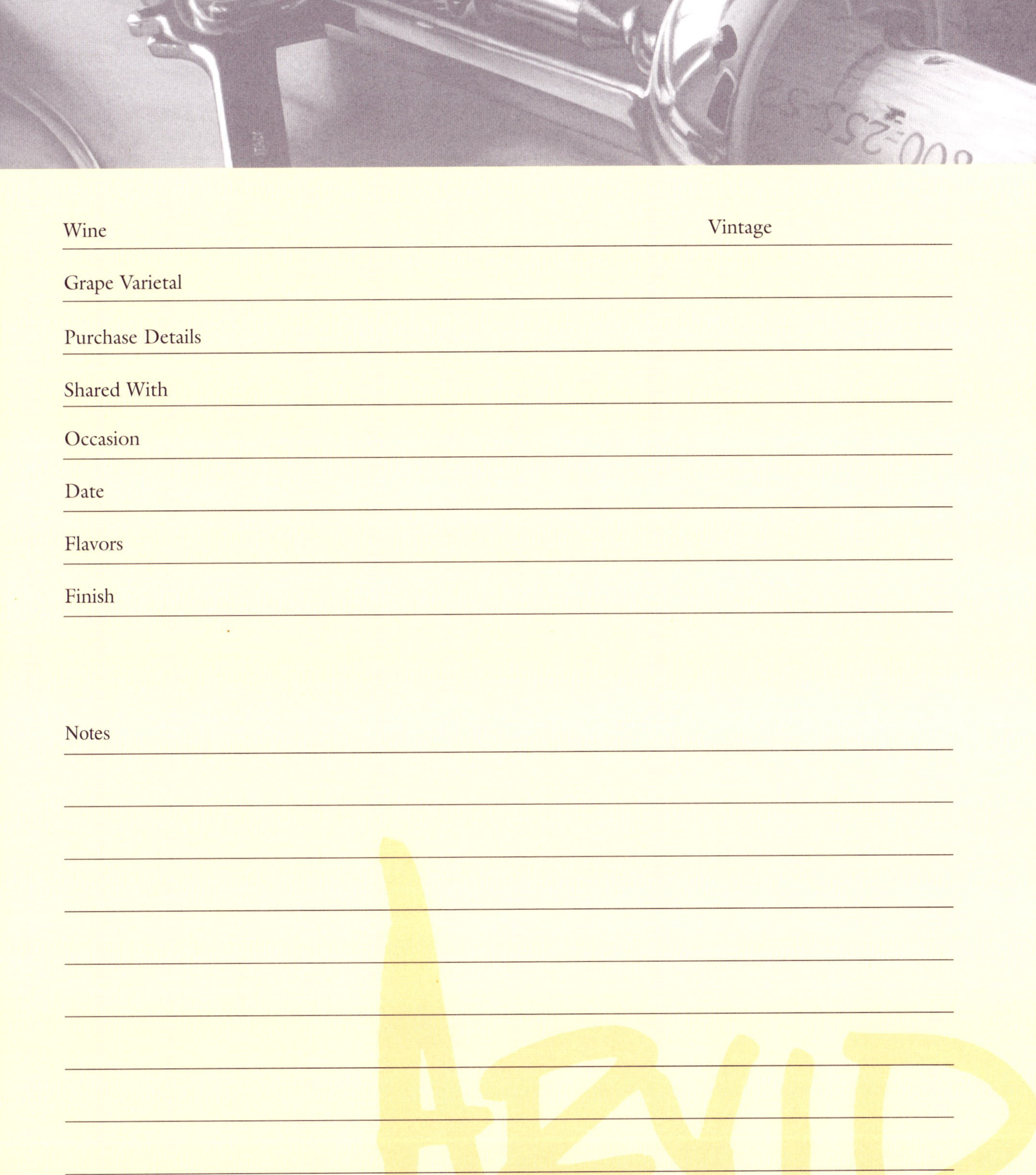

Wine Vintage

Grape Varietal

Purchase Details

Shared With

Occasion

Date

Flavors

Finish

Notes

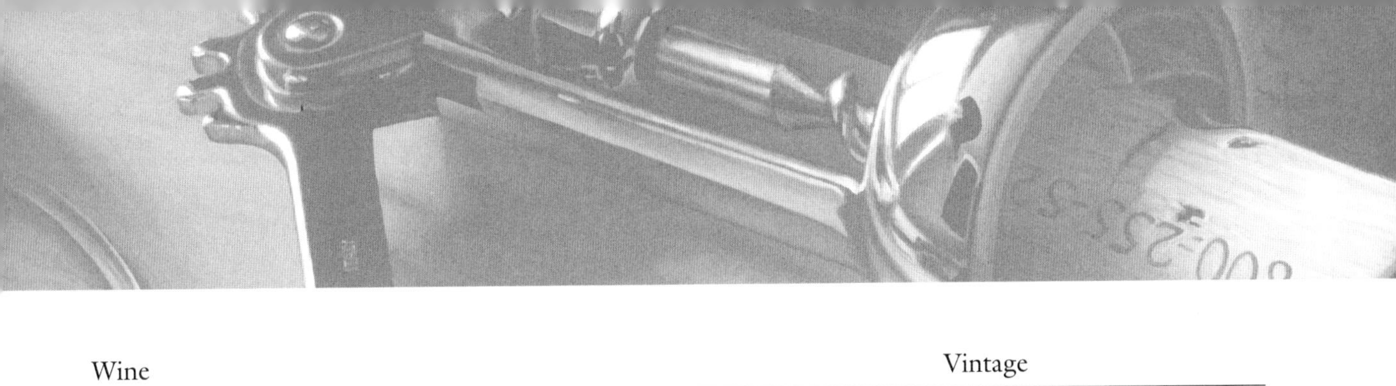

Wine   Vintage

Grape Varietal

Purchase Details

Shared With

Occasion

Date

Flavors

Finish

Notes

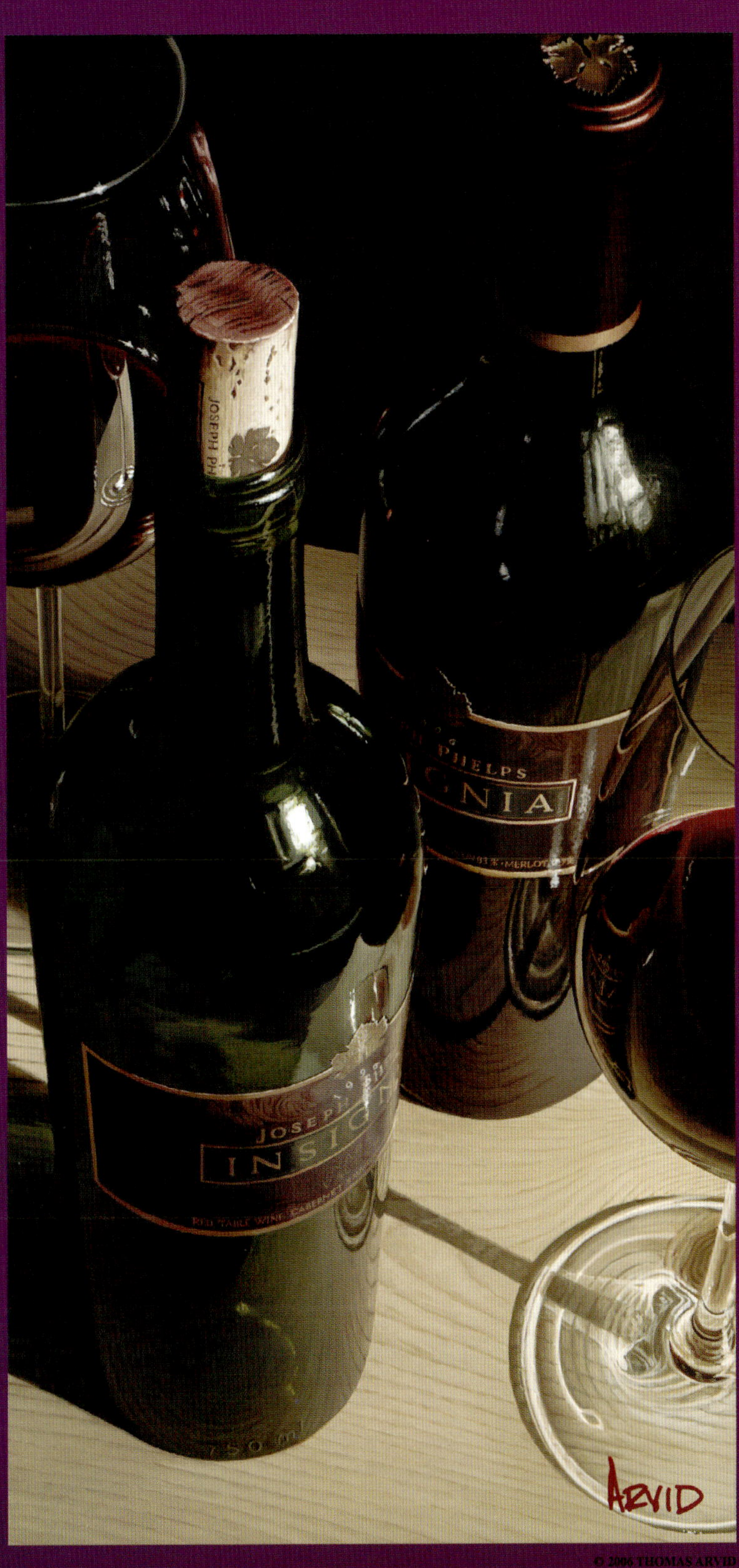

Right Place, Right Time

Right Place, Right Time celebrates the times when great friends get together to share a special bottle of wine. Arvid explains: "When you buy a special bottle of wine you always look forward to the time when you'll open it – who will be there, where you'll be. An amazing bottle is as much about whom you're with as the wine itself; it's about being in the right place, at the right time."

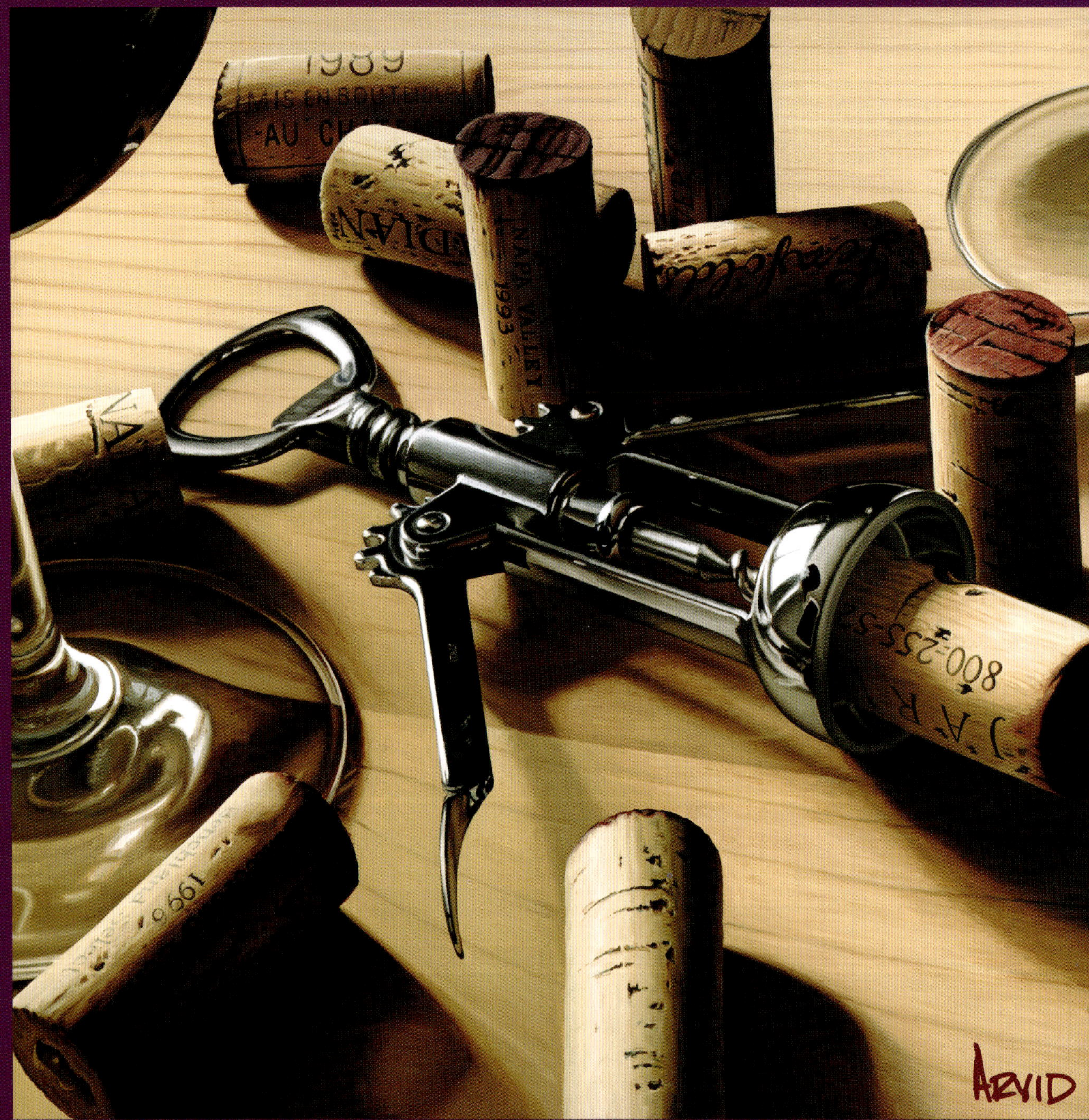

Unplugged

In this seemingly chaotic arrangement of corks, Arvid illustrates his mastery of composition. Capturing the randomly scattered corks in a balance of texture, color, and detail, Arvid introduces us to the world of wine in a way that is both extraordinary and accessible.

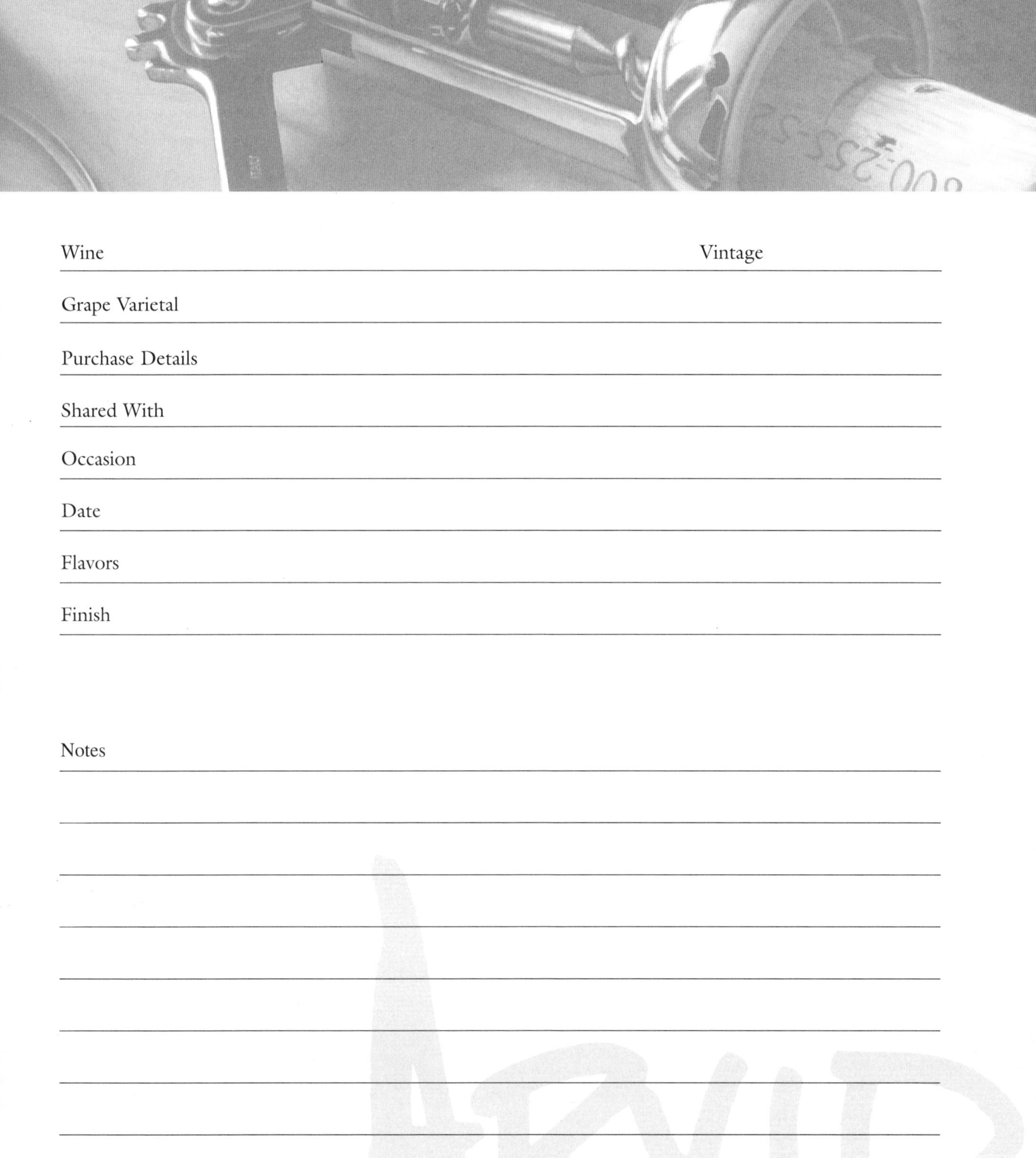

Wine Vintage

Grape Varietal

Purchase Details

Shared With

Occasion

Date

Flavors

Finish

Notes

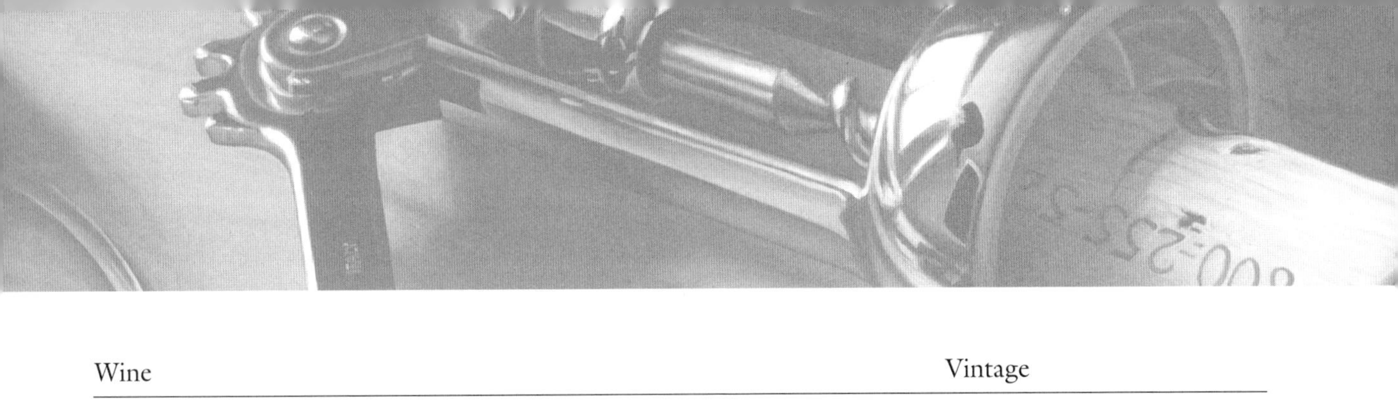

Wine Vintage

Grape Varietal

Purchase Details

Shared With

Occasion

Date

Flavors

Finish

Notes

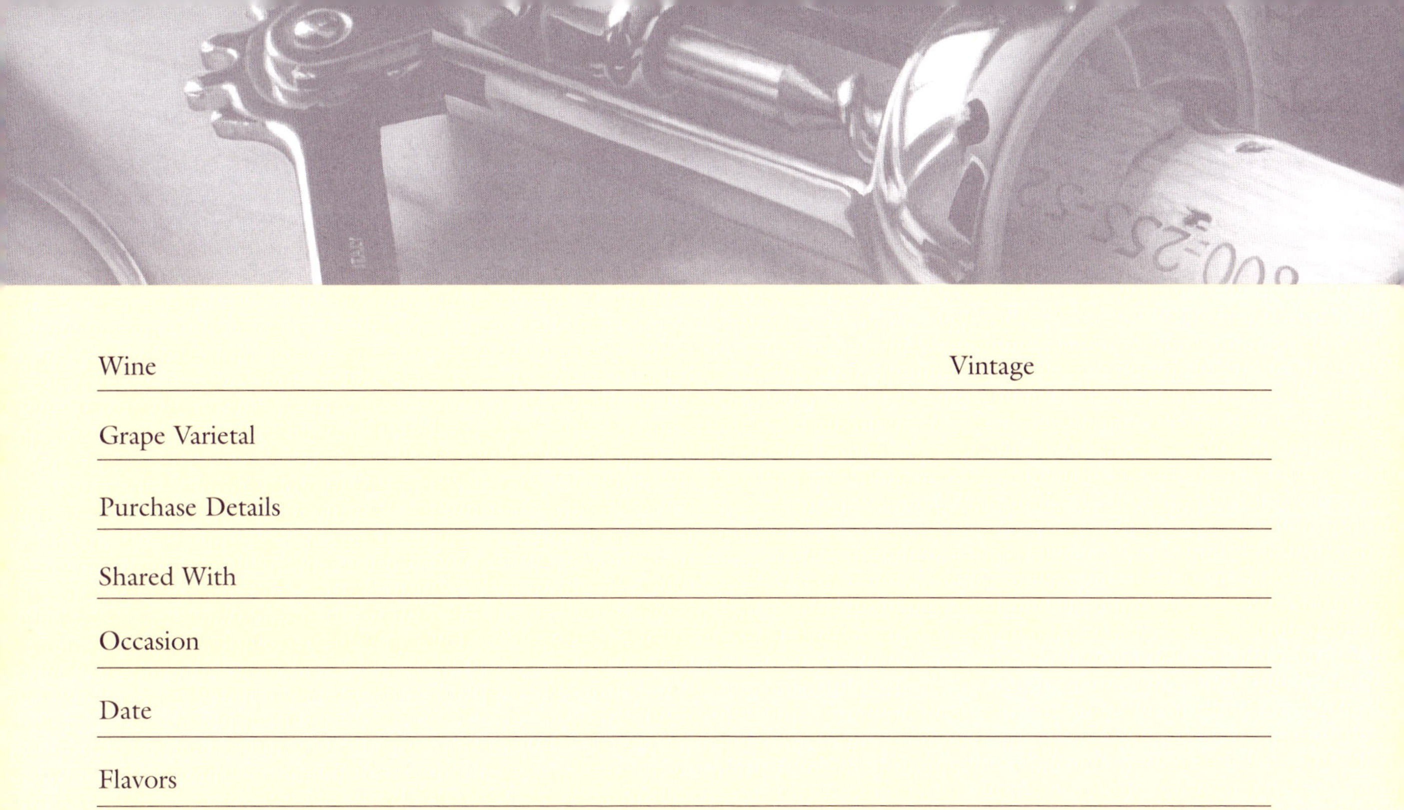

Wine Vintage

Grape Varietal

Purchase Details

Shared With

Occasion

Date

Flavors

Finish

Notes

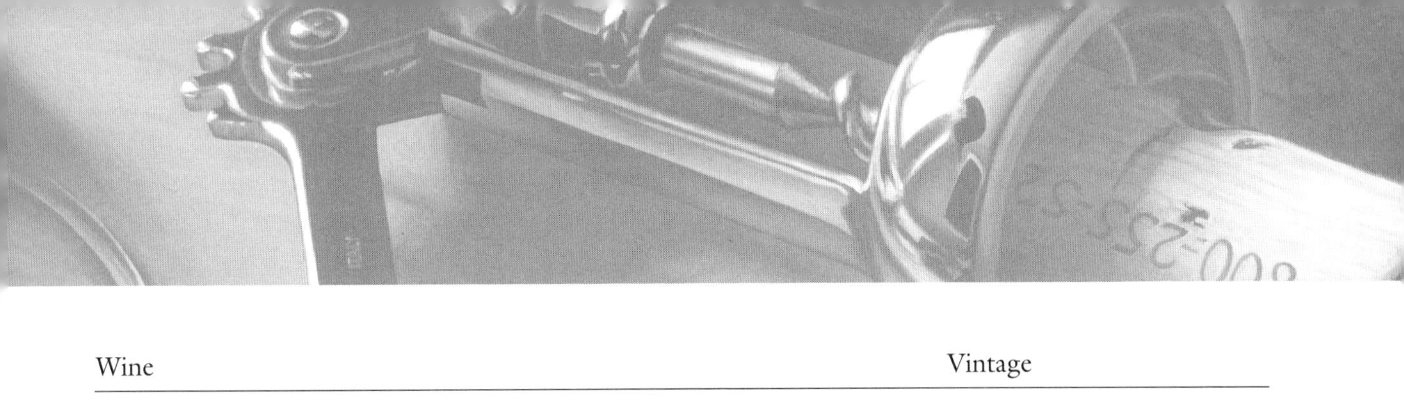

Wine Vintage

Grape Varietal

Purchase Details

Shared With

Occasion

Date

Flavors

Finish

Notes

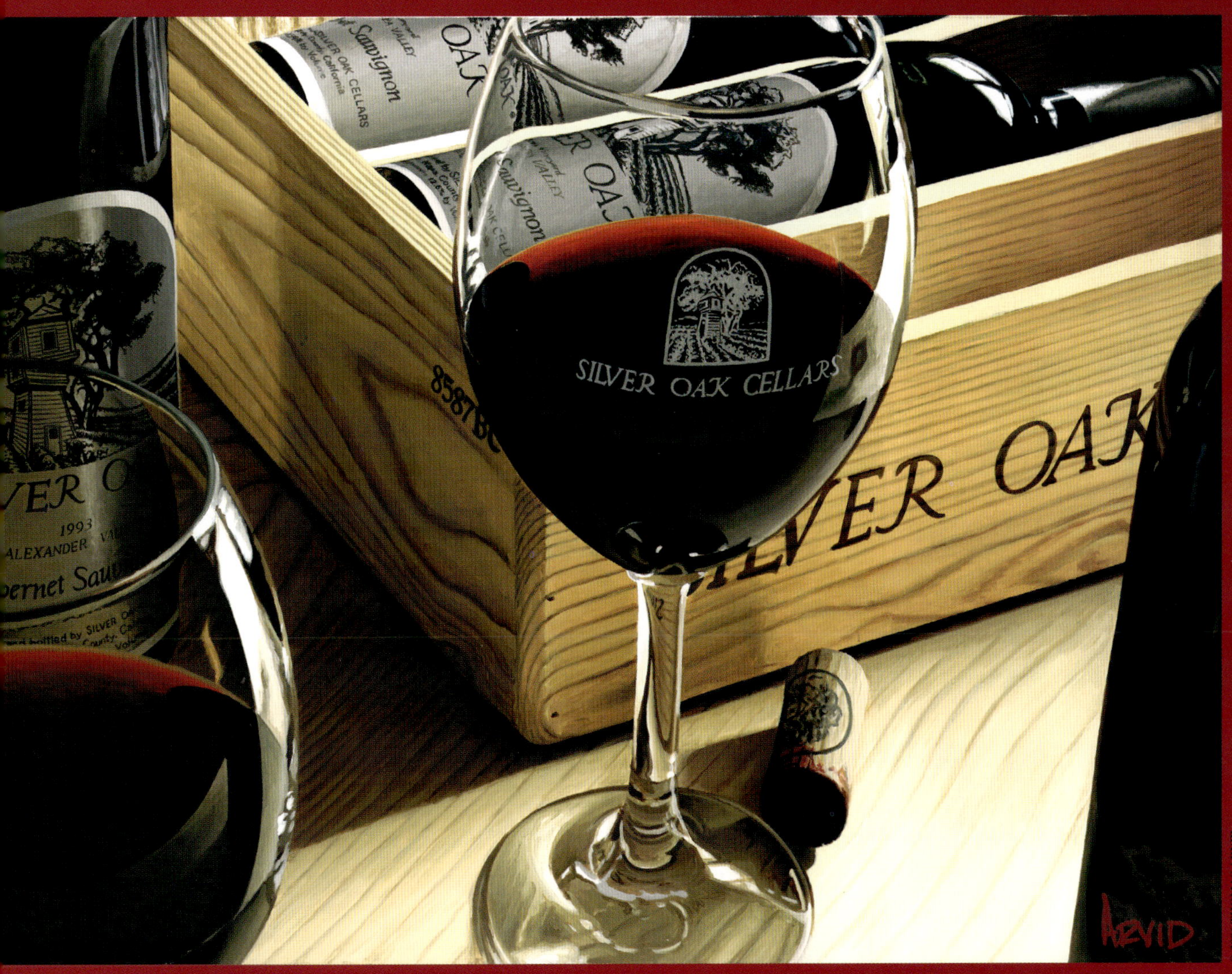

A Well Stocked Cellar

"The artist and the winemaker are visionaries, each in his own medium. One conveys his vision to canvas, the other inside a bottle. The art of painting wine and making wine are all about romance and perception. Good wine is quality art for the heart and soul." *—Arvid*

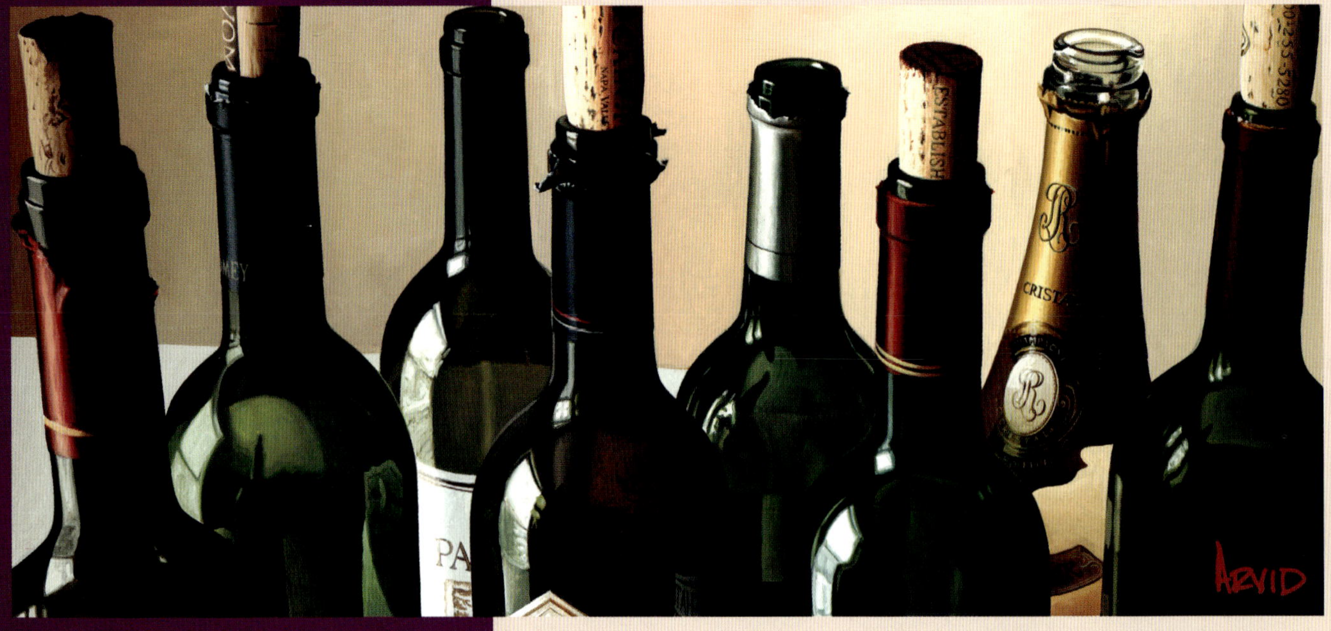

Eight Empties

"*Eight Empties* celebrates an evening of sharing wine and conversation. The composition reflects a spontaneous moment, the gathering of a set of bottles shared and emptied among friends."

—*Arvid*

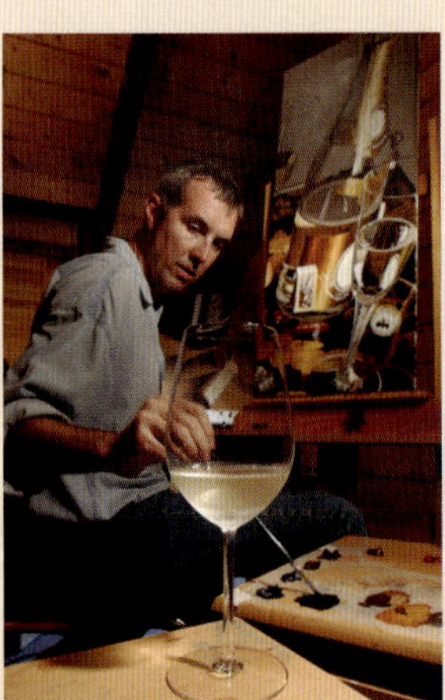

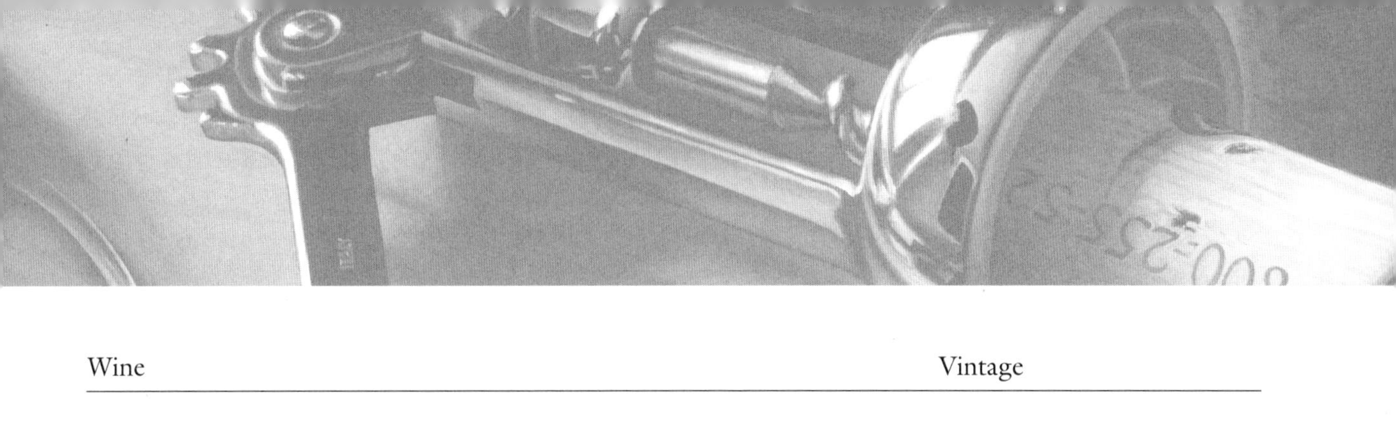

Wine Vintage

Grape Varietal

Purchase Details

Shared With

Occasion

Date

Flavors

Finish

Notes

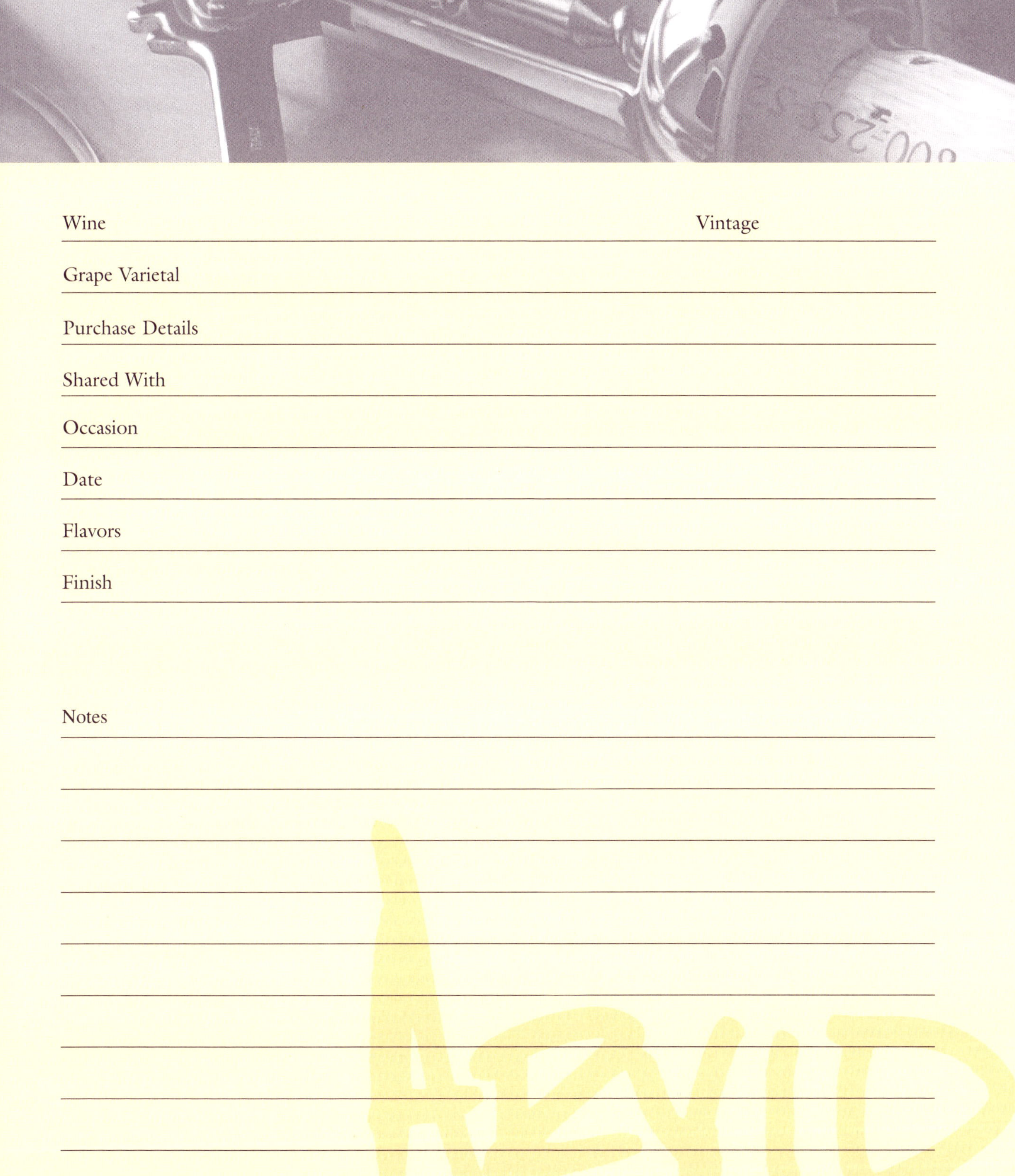

Wine Vintage

Grape Varietal

Purchase Details

Shared With

Occasion

Date

Flavors

Finish

Notes

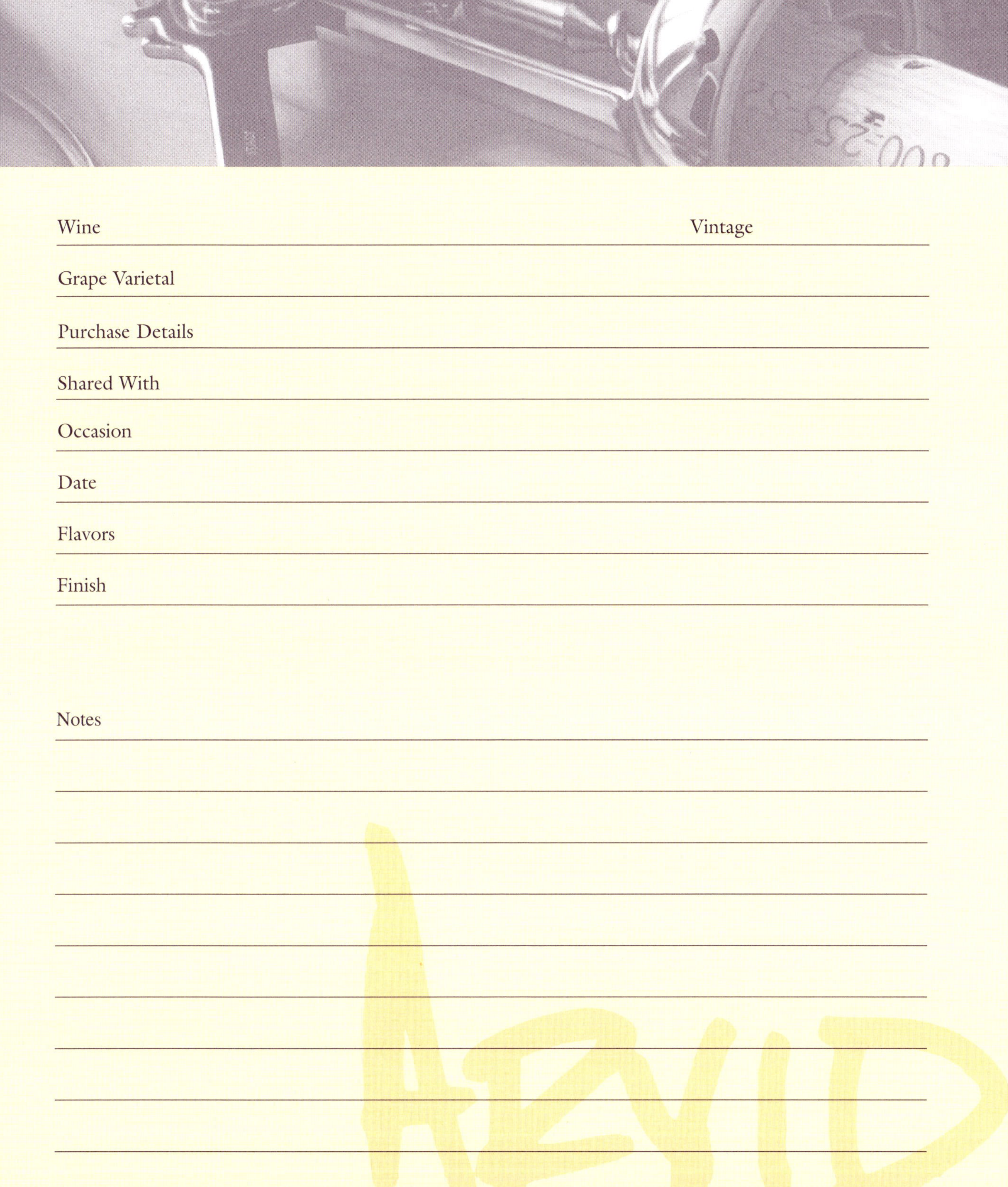

Wine Vintage

Grape Varietal

Purchase Details

Shared With

Occasion

Date

Flavors

Finish

Notes

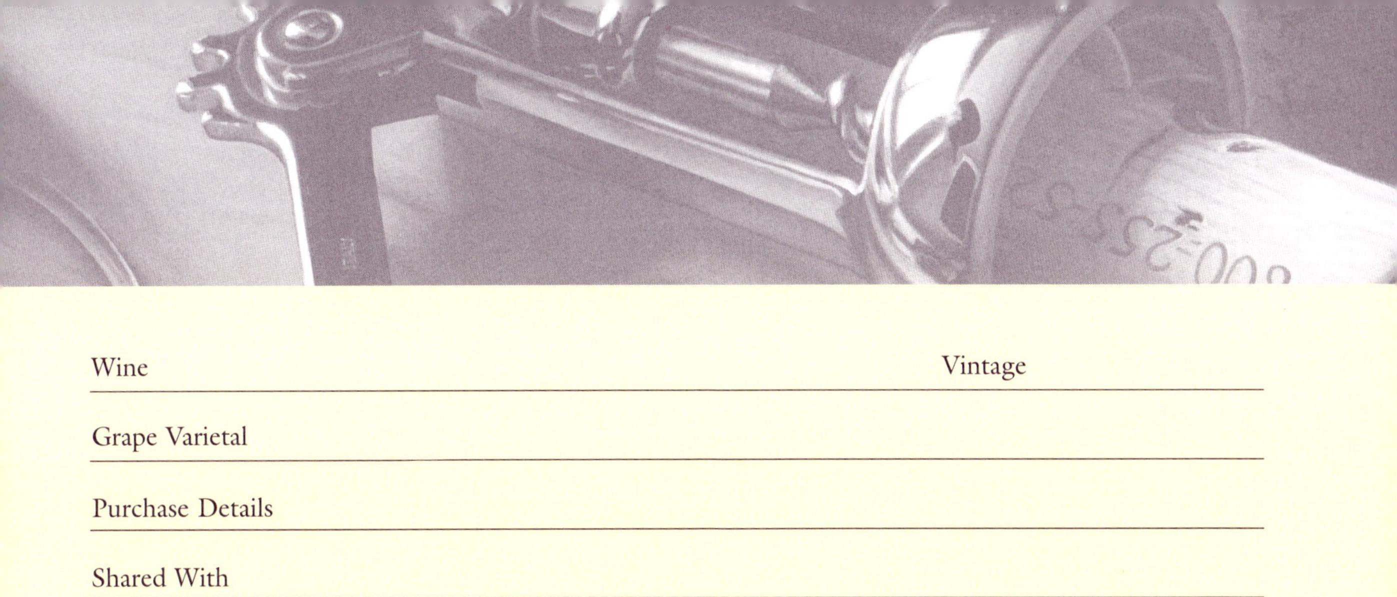

Wine Vintage

Grape Varietal

Purchase Details

Shared With

Occasion

Date

Flavors

Finish

Notes

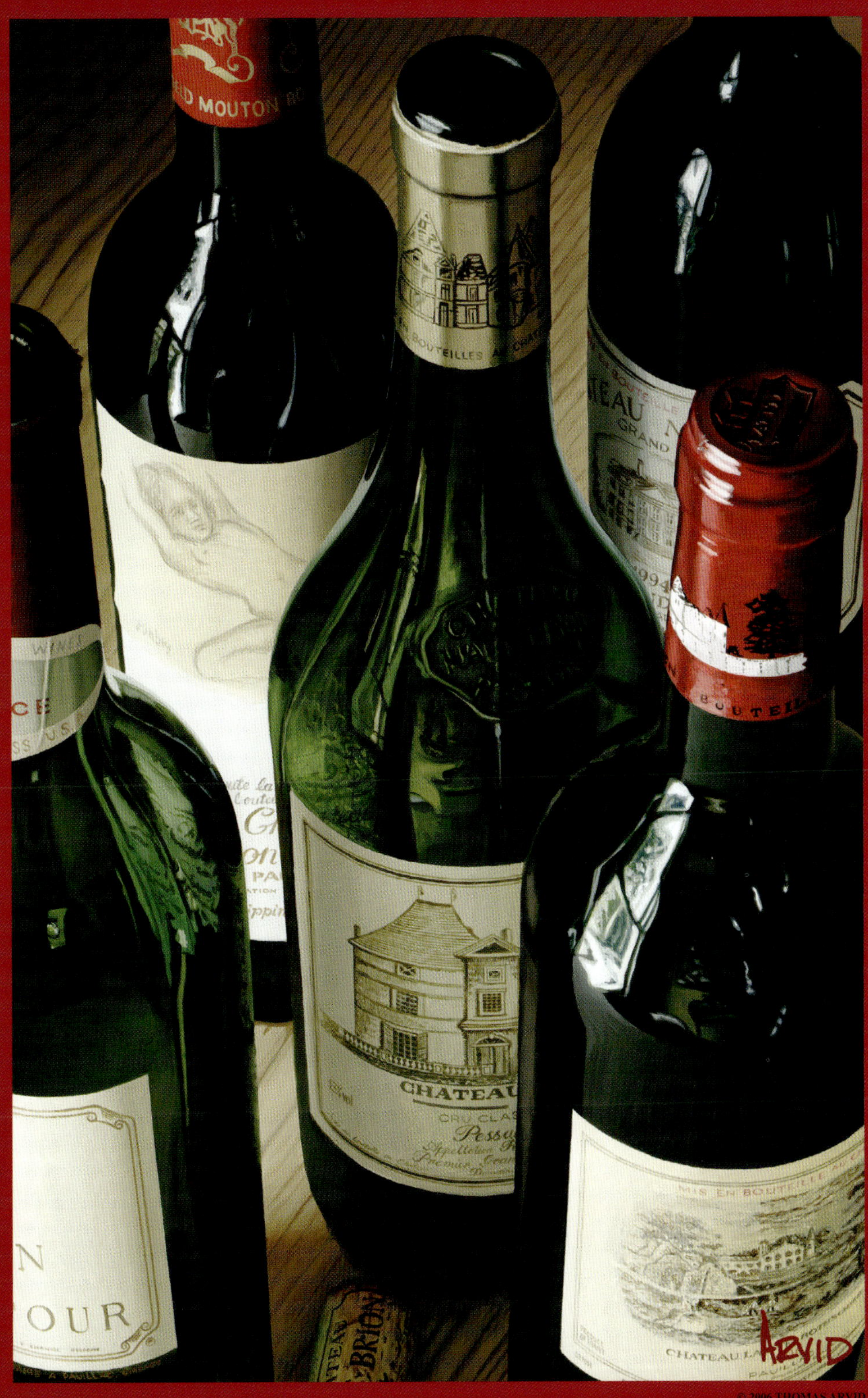

Five First Growths

"When I started, I didn't know much about wine. I would go to the grocery store, buy some red wine and set up a composition. After seeing my grocery selections, someone said, 'Thom, you have to start painting better wines,' and he gave me a great bottle of wine. I remember thinking, 'Wow! Wine tastes like this?' As most artists tend to paint what they know, this is an amazing facet about painting wine—I'm constantly learning more about what I paint." —*Arvid*

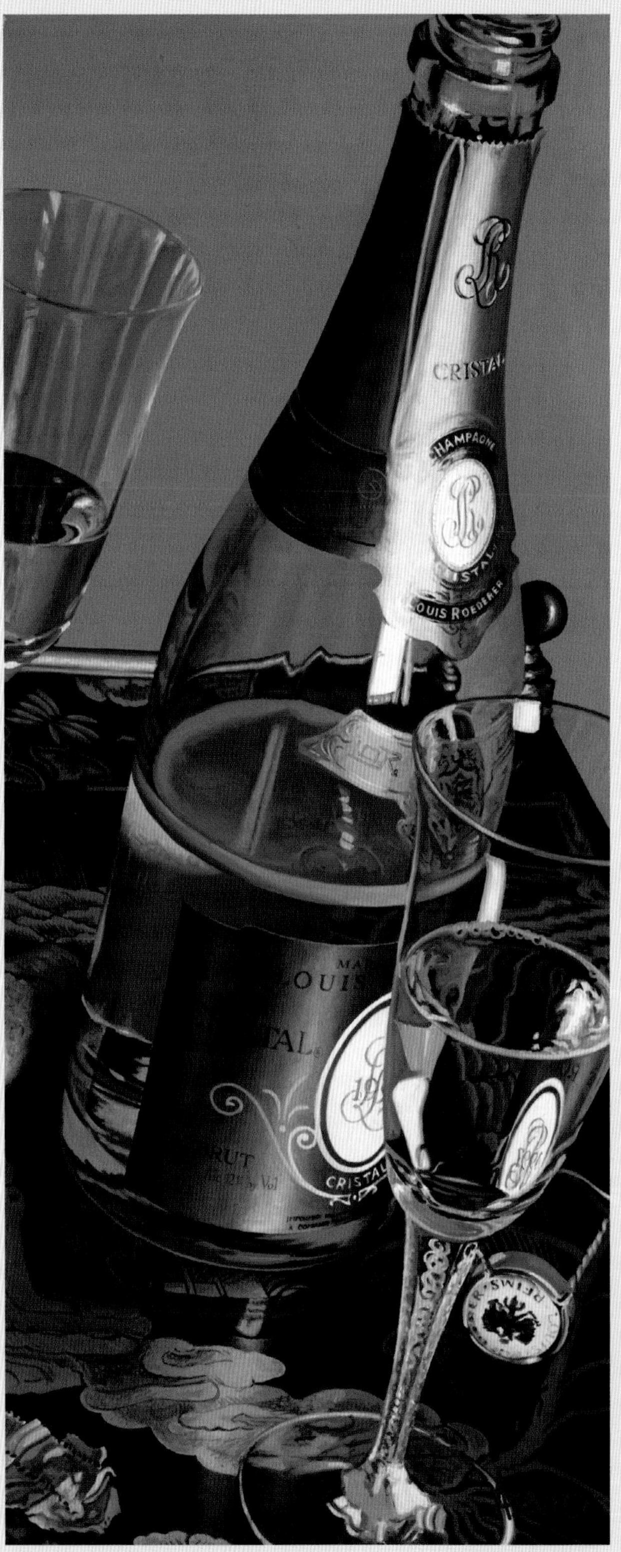

In the Glow

"Great wine has an amazing effect on people. When we're presented with the finer things in life we rise to the occasion; we elevate the everyday to something special, something better. Fine wine makes us slow down and appreciate how beautiful something so simple can be. It's a thought and a way of living that should stay with us every day." *—Arvid*

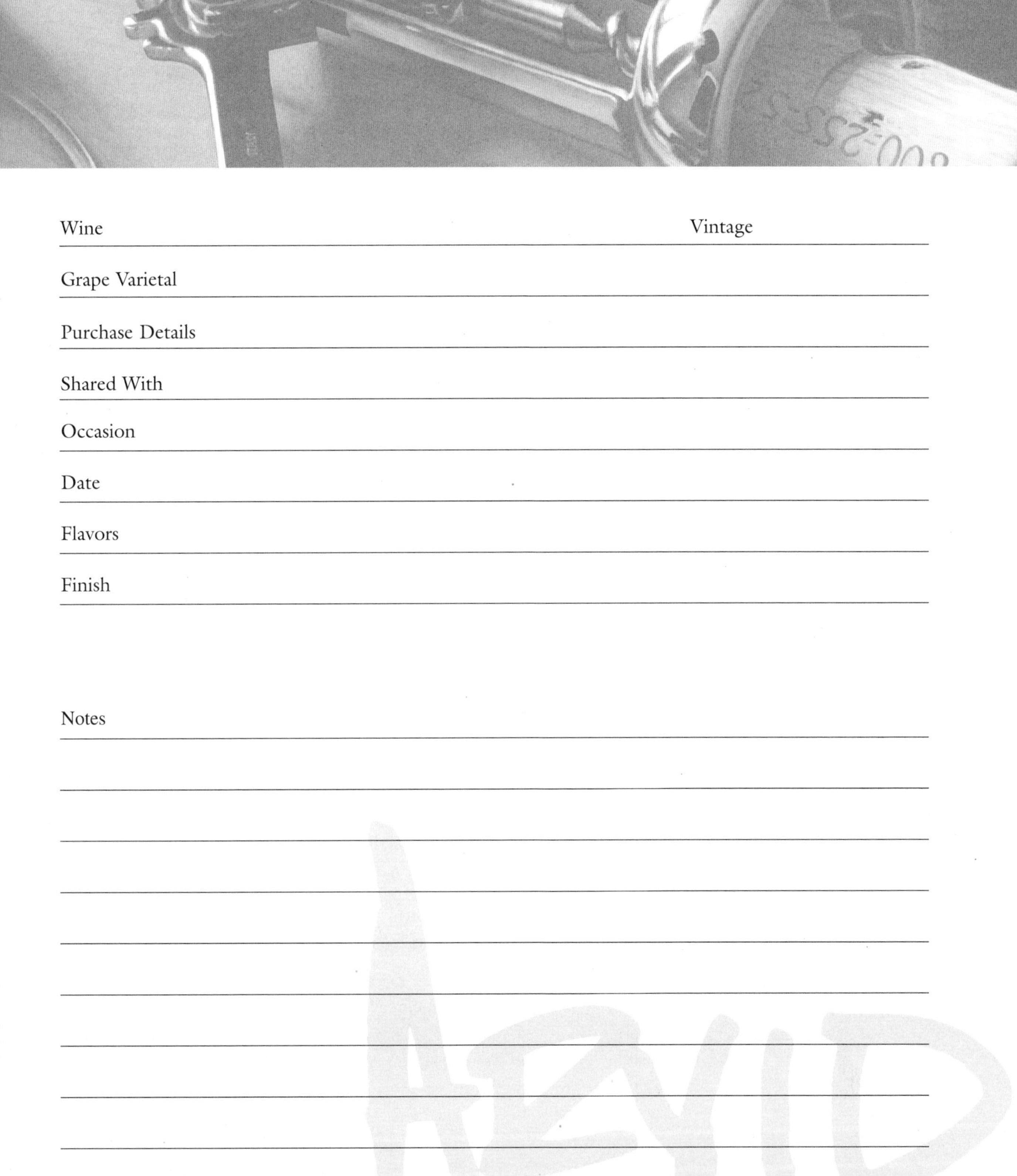

Wine Vintage

Grape Varietal

Purchase Details

Shared With

Occasion

Date

Flavors

Finish

Notes

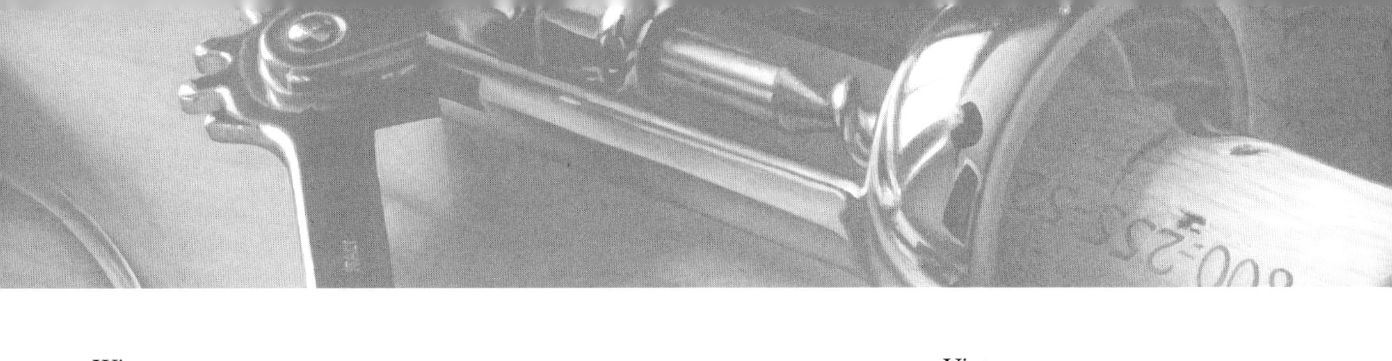

Wine Vintage

Grape Varietal

Purchase Details

Shared With

Occasion

Date

Flavors

Finish

Notes

Wine Vintage

Grape Varietal

Purchase Details

Shared With

Occasion

Date

Flavors

Finish

Notes

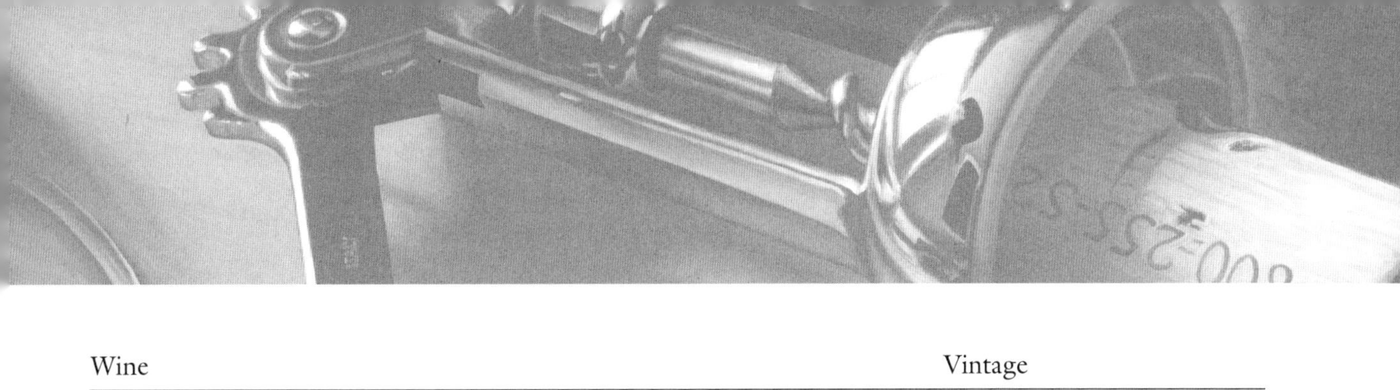

Wine Vintage

Grape Varietal

Purchase Details

Shared With

Occasion

Date

Flavors

Finish

Notes

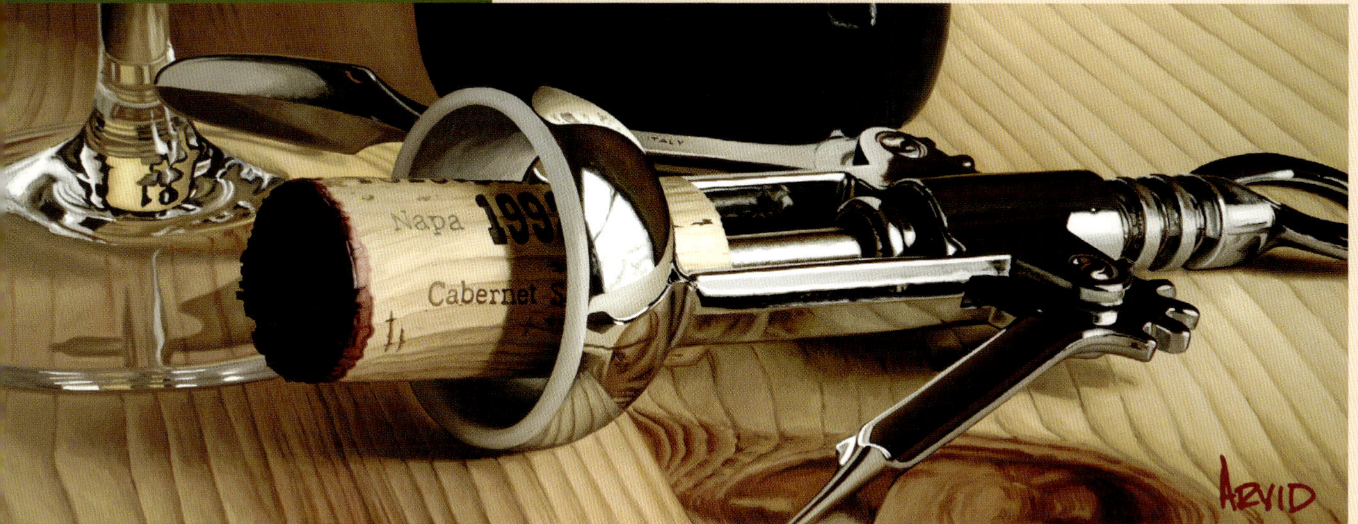

Cork

Cork captures in larger-than-life detail a single element of the wine experience. The hastily discarded cork intrigues us, makes us wonder about the wine that cannot be seen, and invites us to fill a glass of our own.

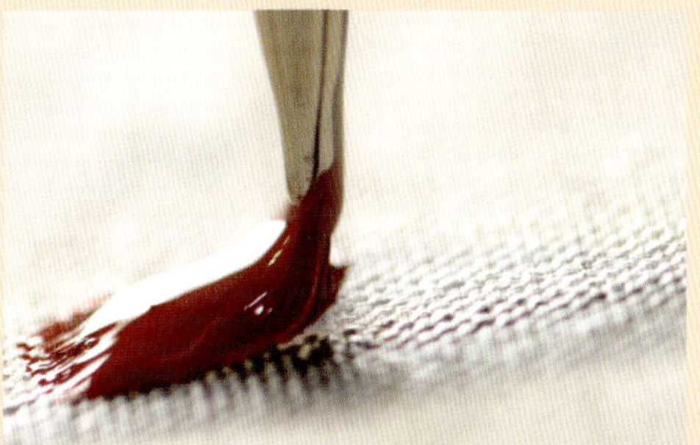

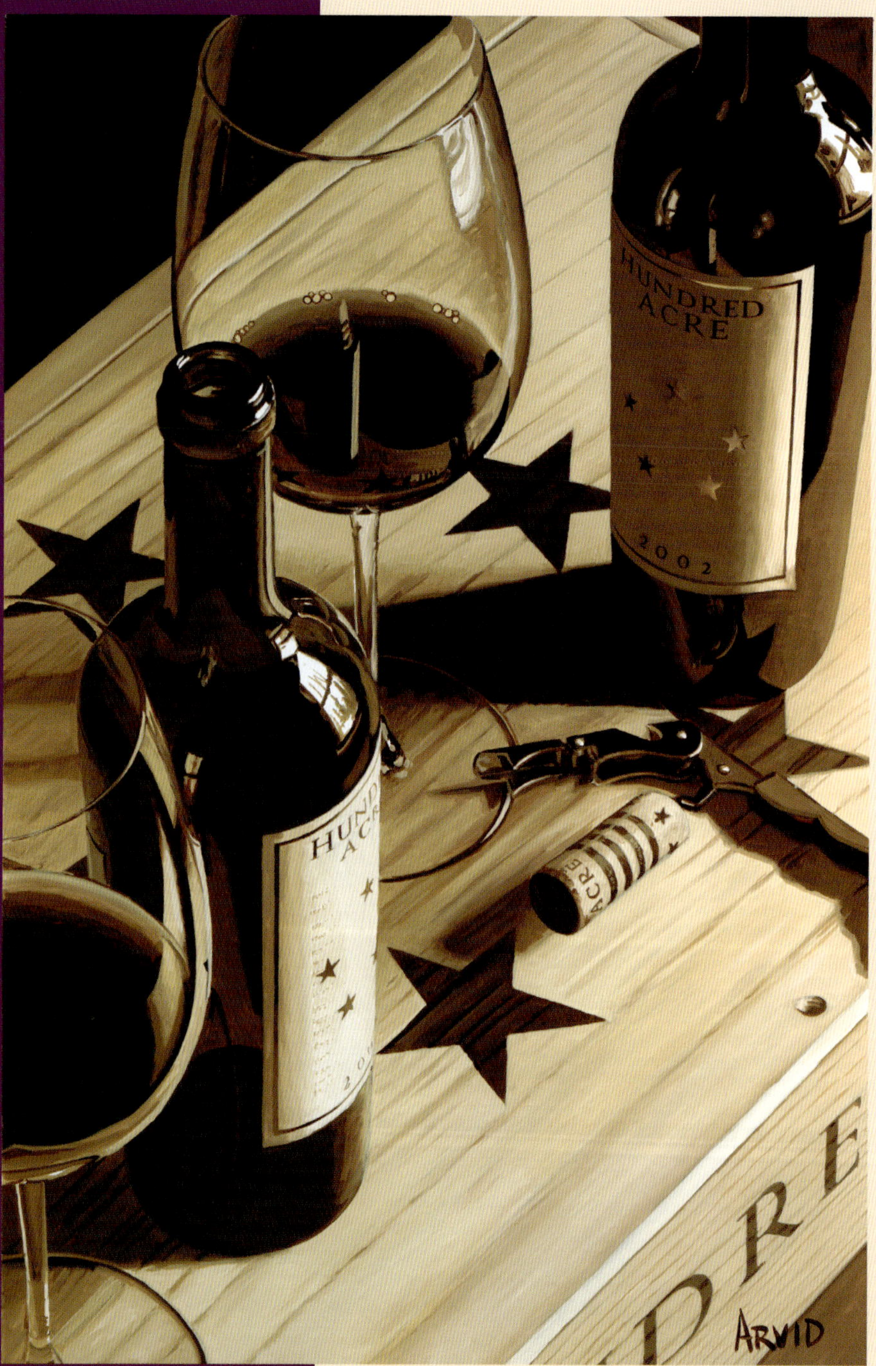

Living Large

Echoing the volume and intensity of big wines, *Living Large* is a monument that celebrates bold ventures. The sharp angles and brazen curves in this oversize composition demand attention. With an eye for detail and beauty, Arvid invites us to share his vision of living life to the fullest.

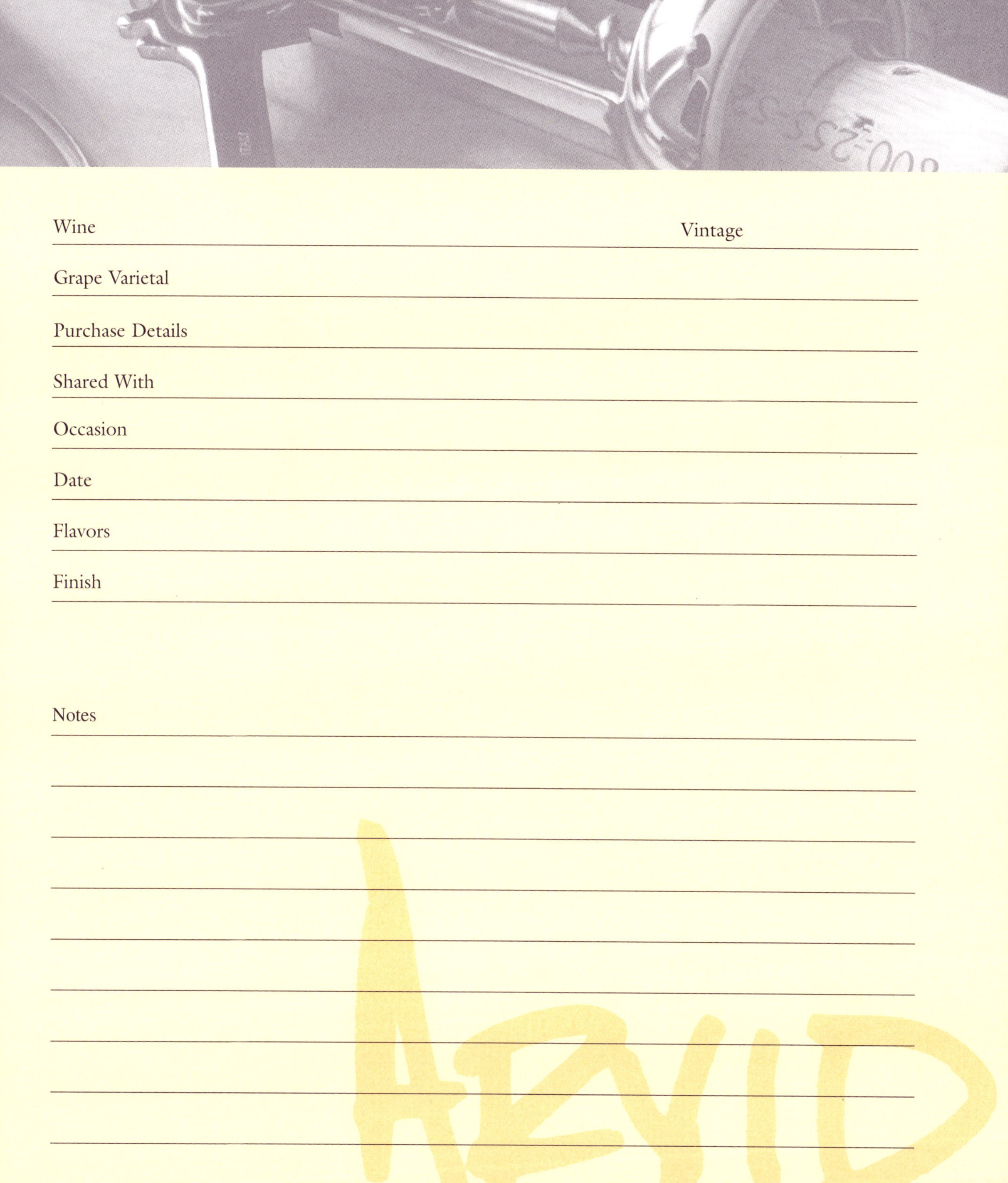

Wine Vintage

Grape Varietal

Purchase Details

Shared With

Occasion

Date

Flavors

Finish

Notes

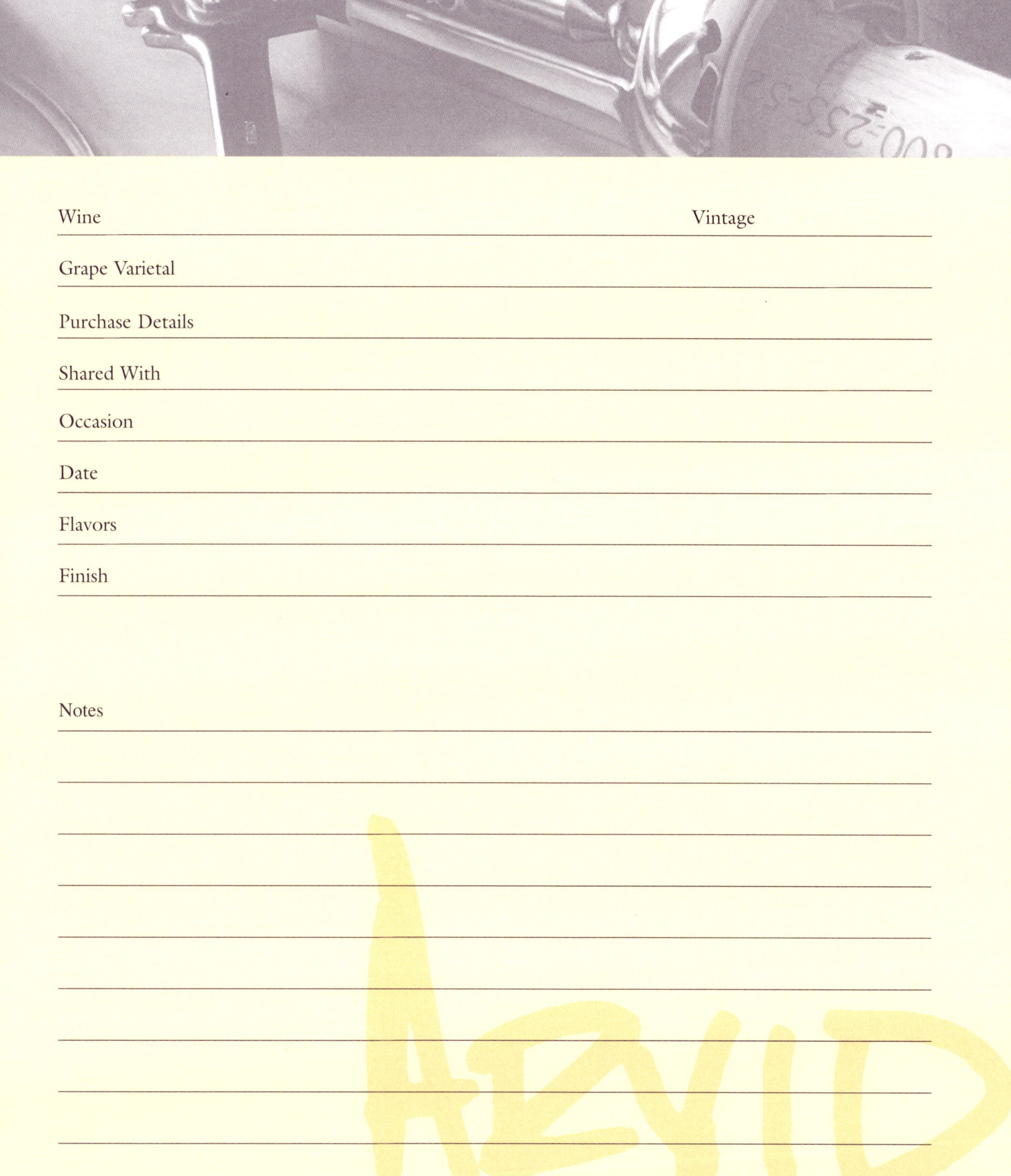

Wine

Vintage

Grape Varietal

Purchase Details

Shared With

Occasion

Date

Flavors

Finish

Notes

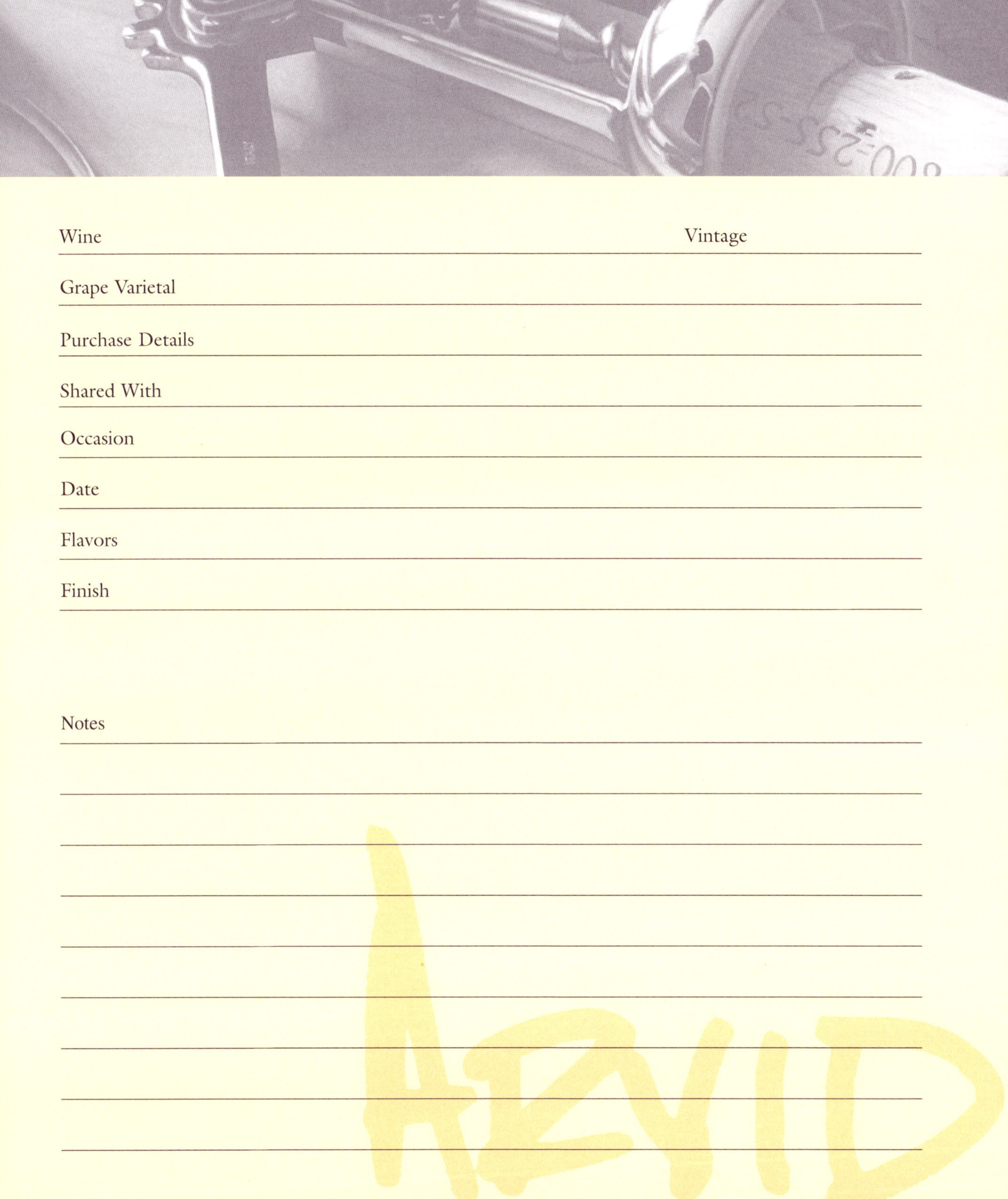

Wine Vintage

Grape Varietal

Purchase Details

Shared With

Occasion

Date

Flavors

Finish

Notes

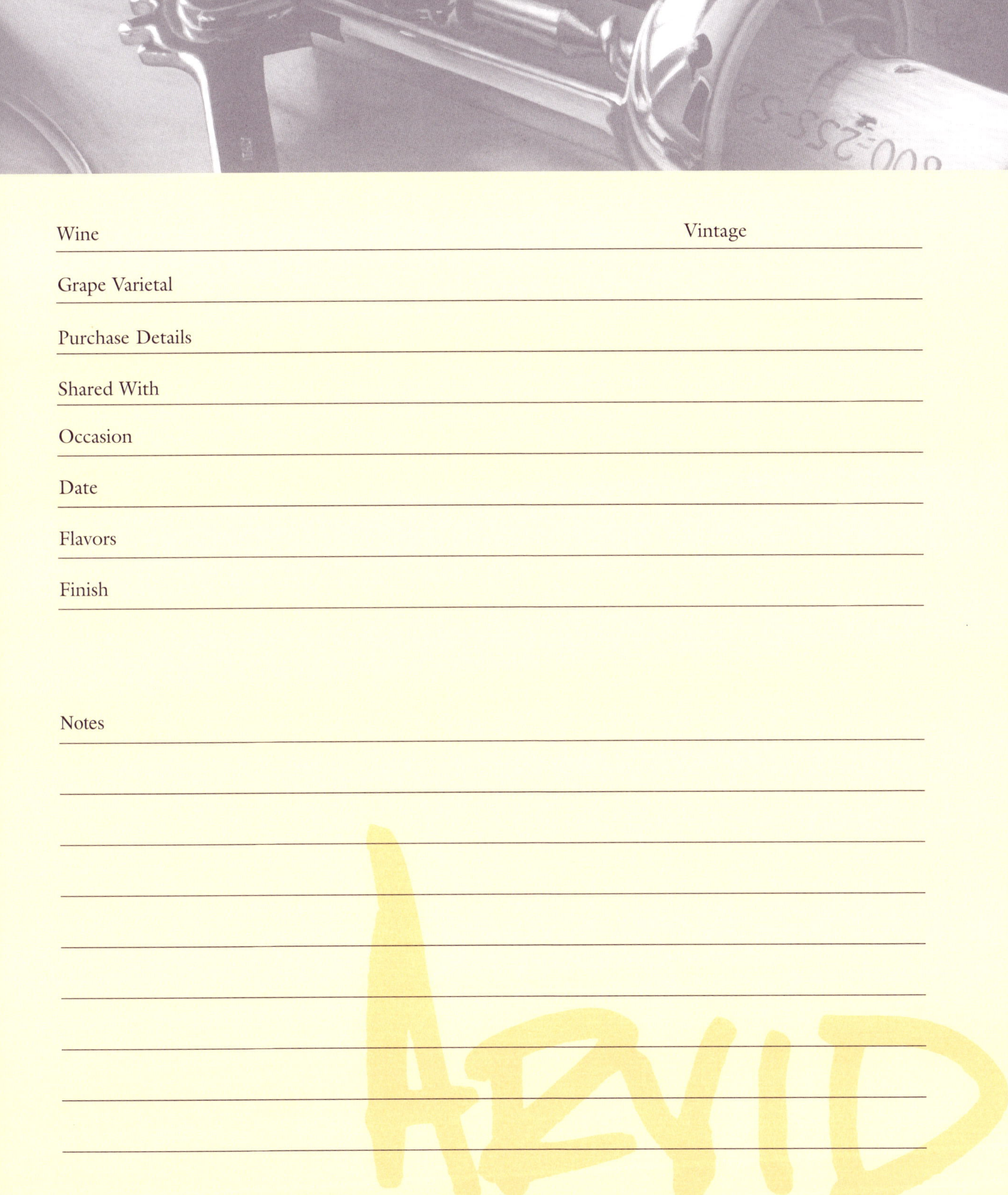

Wine Vintage

Grape Varietal

Purchase Details

Shared With

Occasion

Date

Flavors

Finish

Notes

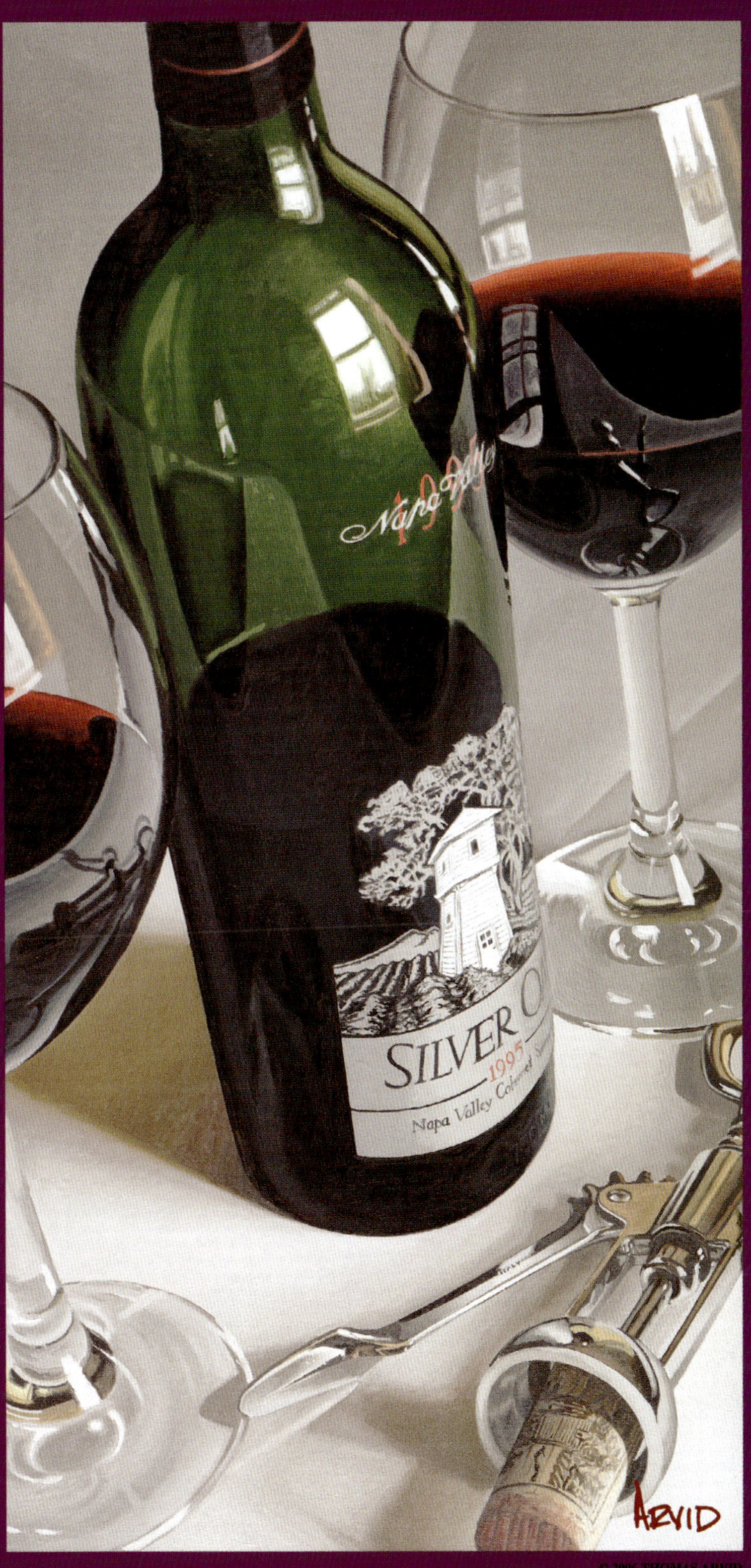

Half Full

"With my paintings, there is never a complete subject: everything is interrupted. I show fragments of things and your mind creates the rest of the image. I think that a lot of the strength of my work lies in that idea. People become connected to a piece that lets them create the area around it. Wine is a great subject to do this with because it is familiar. You know it, so your mind fills in the composition with your own experience. It becomes the viewer's painting too." *—Arvid*

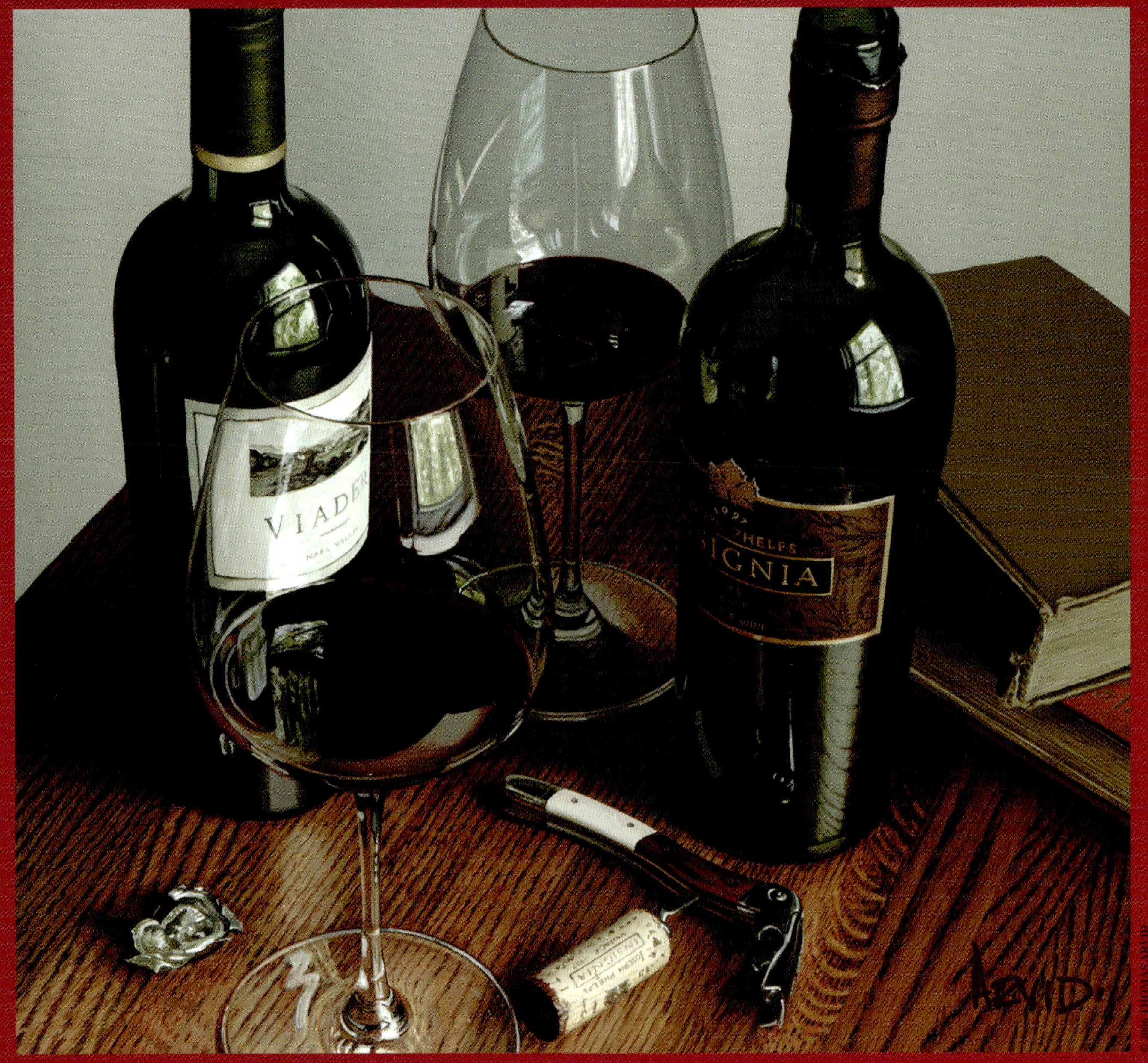

Cover to Cover

With a fresh twist on his definitive style, Arvid continues to astonish in *Cover to Cover.* Warm and inviting, the meticulous detail of the wood, worn fiber of the book and intricate reflections of the glass beg us to join this intimate study. Like a literary classic enjoyed over and over again, Arvid's refined skill is timeless.

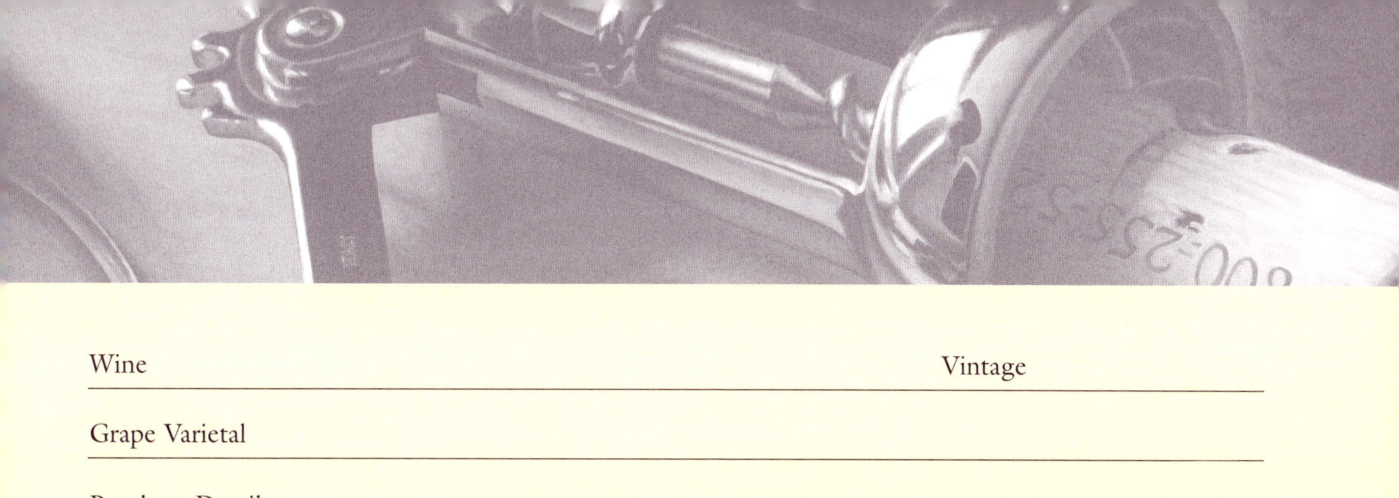

Wine ______________________________ Vintage ____________

Grape Varietal ______________________________

Purchase Details ______________________________

Shared With ______________________________

Occasion ______________________________

Date ______________________________

Flavors ______________________________

Finish ______________________________

Notes ______________________________

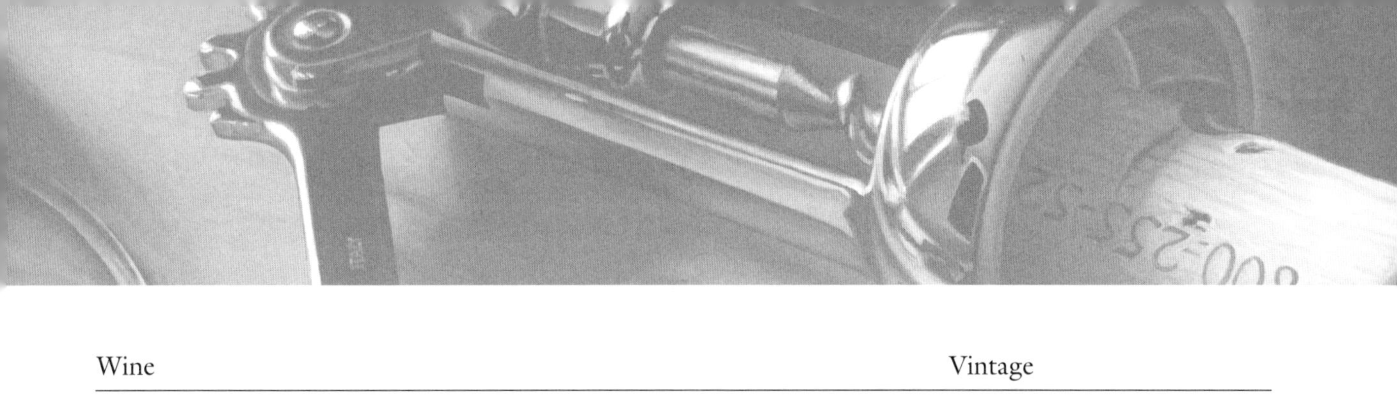

Wine Vintage

Grape Varietal

Purchase Details

Shared With

Occasion

Date

Flavors

Finish

Notes

CRISTAL

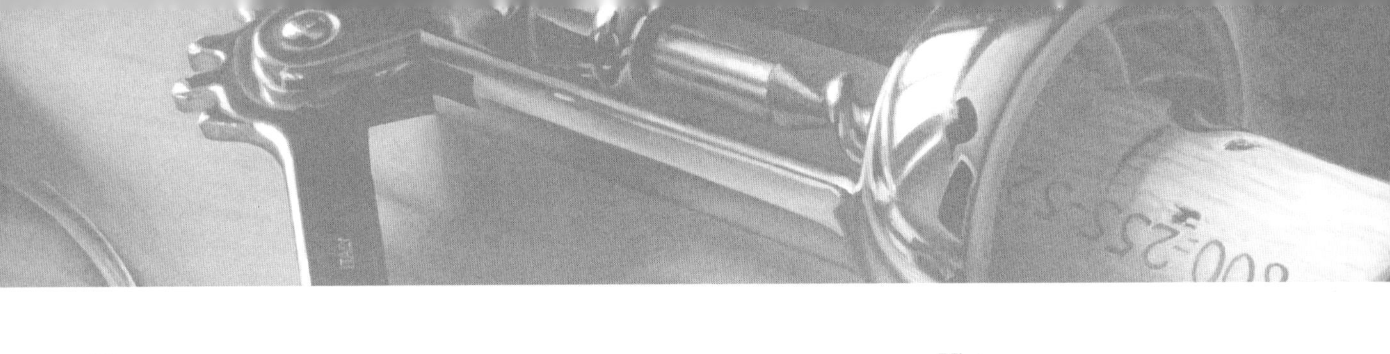

Wine Vintage

Grape Varietal

Purchase Details

Shared With

Occasion

Date

Flavors

Finish

Notes

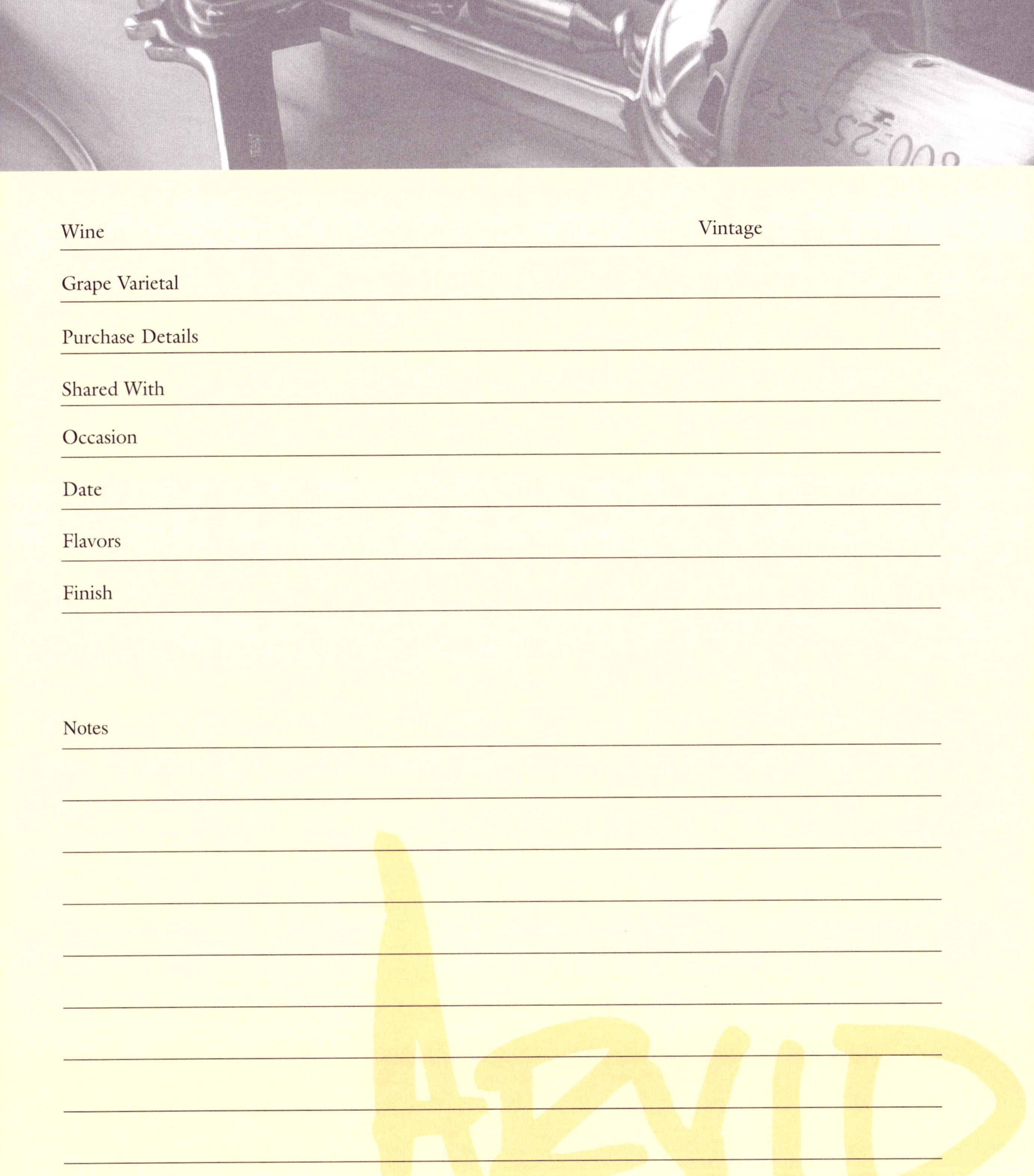

Wine Vintage

Grape Varietal

Purchase Details

Shared With

Occasion

Date

Flavors

Finish

Notes

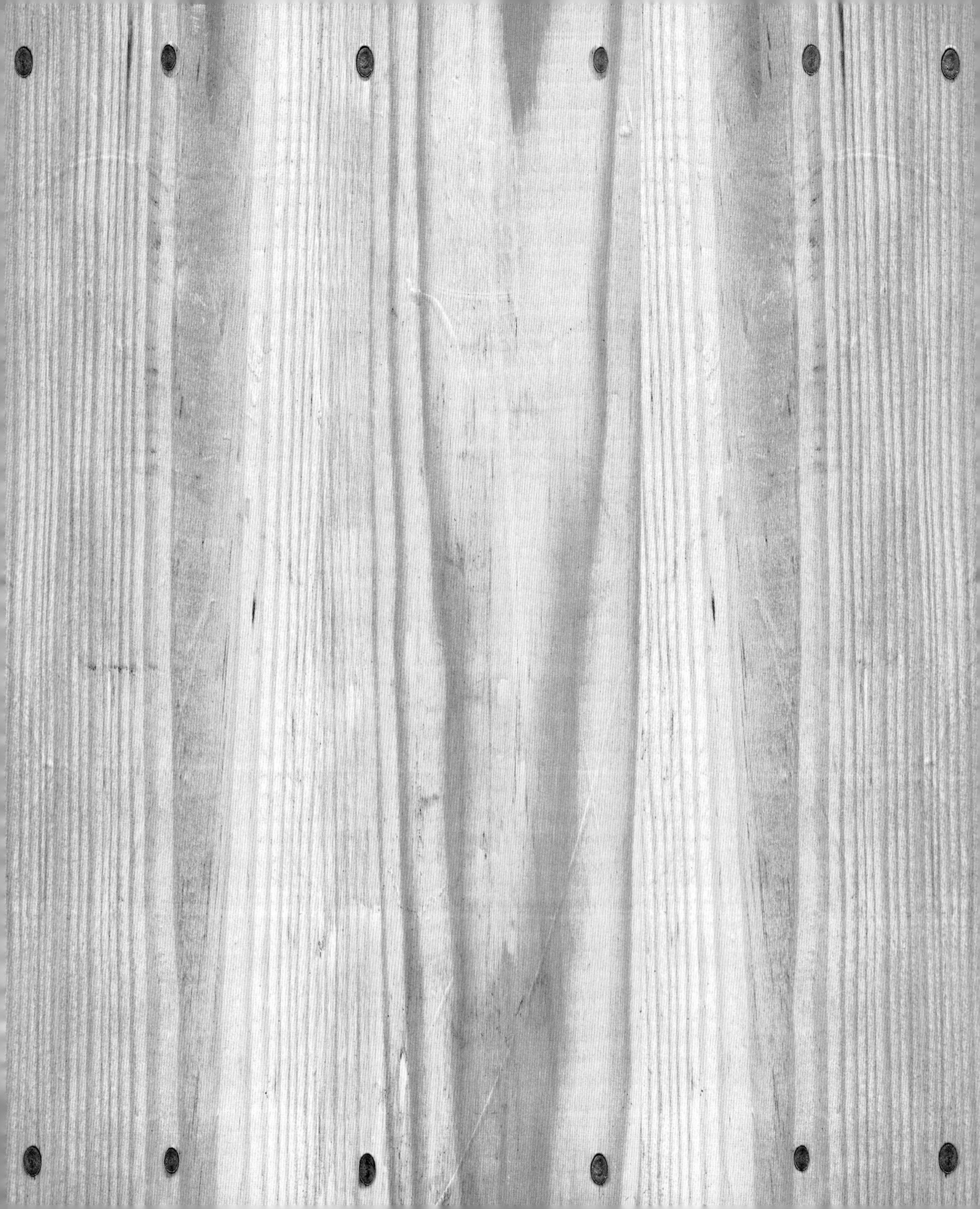